Fly Patterns of Northern New Mexico

Fly Patterns

of Northern New Mexico

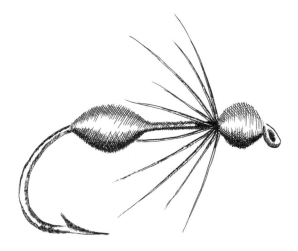

Karen Denison and Bill Orr

University of New Mexico Press ■ Albuquerque

Library of Congress Cataloging-in-Publication Data

Denison, Karen, 1959–
Fly patterns of northern New Mexico / Karen Denison and
    Bill Orr.—
1st ed.
      p. cm.
      ISBN 0-8263-2030-9 (paper : alk. paper)
      1. Flies, Artificial—New Mexico. 2. Fly tying—New
Mexico. I. Orr, Bill, 1960– II. Title.
SH451 .D448 2000
688.7'9124'09789—dc21
                                                99-050498

Cover illustration: Line fly illustrations by William Orr,
    background photo by Karen Denison, and fish photo
    by Mitchell McCorcle.
Text illustration: Line fly illustrations by William Orr,
    black and white photographs by Mark Nohl.

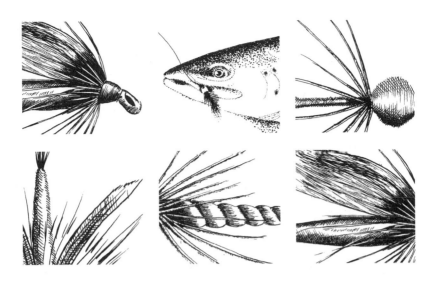

Contents

Disclaimer/Acknowledgment

Although we have tried to give credit where credit is due, the tyers whose names are attached to each pattern are the folks who've brought these particular flies to our attention, whether they are the original creator of the pattern or not. Since the craft of fly fishing—and fly tying—has been around for over five hundred years, it seems safe to assume that at least some of today's pattern "discoveries" touted in glossy magazines and elsewhere are actually inadvertent re-creations of flies that have been tied and described elsewhere with small variations introduced. Bill recently tied a series of beadhead flies based upon Japanese patterns over two hundred years old. And we thought beadheads were a new introduction!

The advent of "patented" fly patterns—where a particular tyer's name is linked legally to use of the pattern—seems unfortunate. It promotes the idea that a particular person exclusively "owns" a fly and seems to run contrary to the enjoyable experimentation that fuels most fly tyers.

New materials add another twist to the equation and the liberal use of taper-drilled beads, polypropylene, mylar, and other synthetics has lead to flies that really do differ strikingly from the old patterns.

But whether truly innovative or reinventions of standards, the fly patterns described in this book are reliably useful for this area and fun to tie. To our knowledge, none of these patterns are "patented" nor an exact copy of a widely known standard. A few have been in use in this area long enough to qualify for their own "standard" status although they have not been previously published. And at least one has been published locally, but not in step-by-step format. The unifying theme is: we like these flies and think you will, too. We would like to thank and acknowledge all the people who contributed to the lengthy production of this book, especially those generous tyers who agreed to divulge their favorite patterns. Interacting with these folks is always a wonderful excuse to swap more fish stories and learn new things about fly fishing.

A special debt is also owed to Sangre de Cristo Flyfishers of Santa Fe who self-published a collection of fly patterns for this area in 1992, in an out-of-print booklet "Fly Patterns for Northern New Mexico." Several of the patterns from that booklet have been revisited here, with updates from the individual tyers.

Foreword

The secret—if it ever really was one—is out. Anglers from New York to San Diego have discovered that fly fishing in New Mexico is more than the tailwater on the fabled San Juan River. While some would argue that the sport's expansion is a detriment, I find it exciting that anglers are now listening to the distinctive melodies of New Mexico's small streams.

Besides, when trout become accustomed to fly patterns mixed with natural insects bobbing along the surface, they get "smarter" and more challenging to catch. For anglers that translates into putting a little more thought into each cast and more care into their selection of flies. That's part of the fun of using artificials instead of drowning bait worms, and it permits fly fishers the luxury of repeating the epigram: "The fishing was great, even though the catching wasn't so good."

Since the publication of my *Fly-Fishing in Northern New Mexico* in 1991, local and visiting fly fishers have lamented the lack of a fully descriptive fly pattern book to accompany the where-to guide. Patterns specific to New Mexico waters have been around since the late 1940s, but until now no one bothered to collect them in a comprehensive reference. I'm delighted that the void is finally filled by two highly-skilled, well-respected anglers and fly tyers, Karen Denison and Bill Orr.

While researching a little book on the Rio Grande, I spent a hot April afternoon interviewing and fishing with one of New Mexico's legendary guides. After working our way along a quarter-mile stretch of the river below Pilar and coming up with more sunburn than trout, we retreated to a bluff overlooking a long stretch of water. As we talked of how the river was as moody as our first girlfriends, an angler worked through the stretch below our perch. When the fly fisher landed a third fish in the space of five minutes, my companion sat up and paid more attention.

"Damn good fisherman," he commented as he studied the way the angler patiently spotted the next cast. A couple more fish followed and, as the angler came closer, I recognized the magenta waders and stylish hat. The guide stared intently before suddenly jumping up and exclaiming, "My God, it's a woman!"

Having started his illustrious career when it was uncommon to find both sexes on the water, I think he was astonished that one of those female upstarts had so blatantly outfished us. That angler was Karen Denison and being shown up by her was no surprise. Karen is widely regarded as one of northern New Mexico's most notable anglers.

The fly tying wizardry of Bill Orr first came to my attention ten years ago at meetings of the Sangre de Cristo Fly Fishers. The club's monthly raffle usually included a dozen flies tied by Bill. These insect imitations always attracted a crowd of gawkers, each of whom marveled at the detailed craftsmanship that went into each pattern. When a club member's number was drawn and the prize was one of my books, the winner politely smiled as he picked up his booty; when he went home with a handful of Bill's flies, the recipient grinned from ear to ear.

It's not unusual to find anglers who believe that a dozen standard patterns are all you need to catch fish in the southern Rockies, so some may question the need for a fly pattern book specific to northern New Mexico. But Karen and Bill field-tested a small flotilla of patterns and included only those that came up winners on regional waters. Rather than a random selection of a couple of tyers' personal favorites, this book offers a genuinely useful collection of flies.

There's something here for everyone, from tailwater junkies, to Rio Grande anglers, to small-stream enthusiasts. It's good to see classic New Mexico dries—like Van Beacham and Jack Woolley's Ginger Dun and Bert and Marie Tallant's Hare's Ear Trude—finding their way back into print. Even hopelessly devoted dry-fly anglers such as myself find it difficult to argue with Bill's legendary success with nymphs, and the reader should pay attention to every word in the subsurface section. Streamers, notably those designed especially for fall trips on the Rio Grande, are given their due, and including a few wet flies in your box will be a welcome addition to your arsenal.

The cryptic names of the fly patterns commonly used on the San Juan River sound like secret code devised to keep outsiders in the dark. The names RS2, WD-40 and others don't mean a thing to anglers not well versed in the lore of the river. Karen and Bill provide San Juan anglers with a compilation of the best patterns for the state's most finicky rainbows. Many aren't much more than a strand of fur on a bare hook, but these sparse patterns regularly produce rod-bending trout below Navajo Dam.

The real test of a fly pattern book is sitting down at the bench and making sense of the recipes and tying instructions. In this case, Bill's expertise as an artist with fur, feathers, and thread pays off for the reader. My clumsy fingers assembled about 20 patterns from Karen and Bill's collection without a hitch. The tying descriptions are not only clear but they anticipate problem spots and guide you through them. Many of the flies are more complex than those I usually attempt, but the detailed, accurate writing in the instructions glued me to the chair for many enthusiastic hours at the tying bench.

Just as valuable as the descriptions of the flies—and perhaps for many anglers more so—are the accompanying paragraphs on when, where, and how to fish the patterns. They remind me of the times I've wandered into a fly shop and listened to Karen and Bill tell me a couple fishing stories that later leaped to mind and saved the day when I was on the water, stumped and searching my fly box for an answer.

Every angler and fly tyer should look carefully at the way these patterns were developed and refined through experimentation. Karen and Bill permit us to peek at the development process for fly patterns for specific waters. This is what sets this book apart from others in the genre: two experts show us the way to experiment with our own patterns to fit the conditions, the fish, and the insects of New Mexico waters. And by encouraging us to experiment with these patterns, Karen and Bill force us to think about trout and bugs, which can only result in greater success on the water. You can't make many adjustments to your fishing lure when you use a garlic cheese ball.

So, what are you waiting for? Get over to the tying bench, thumb through these pages to a pattern that is new to you, and start tying. Your effort will undoubtedly be rewarded the next time you cast for trout on some stream or lake in the mountains of New Mexico.

Craig Martin
Los Alamos, New Mexico

Introduction

As a vacation destination and as permanent residence for many fly fishers, our area contains waters of greatly diverse character: small mountain freestone streams delightful to fish in the high summer months, and larger burly rivers like the Rio Grande with its hidden depths and rough canyon rocks. Successful fly fishing often involves having specific knowledge of the insects, forage fish, and other food sources available to gamefish in a particular watershed, and which fly patterns are likely to imitate those food sources. Some of the best, most successful imitations for New Mexico are flies that have been developed locally and are not widely described or sold commercially outside our area. Two guidebooks specifically describe fly fishing destinations within northern New Mexico, but there is no book currently available that describes in any detail fly patterns of local origin and usefulness.

Regional fly pattern books often seem to fall into two categories: those that are composed of fly patterns sought through blind solicitation, or those patterns that derive from a single tyer's imagination. My co-author and I have produced a collection which bridges these two extremes. We have selected approximately fifty patterns proven over time to be useful to northern New Mexico fly fishers from more than thirty locally respected tyers. In this way we have found a rich and varied group of patterns that reflect the diverse approaches to fly fishing and tying inherent in their originators. An appendix provides recipes for additional patterns of special local usefulness, which are "standard" patterns described in previous, widely available tying manuals.

These fly patterns have been organized by fly type: dries, nymphs, wets, and streamers. Midges for the San Juan River tailwater and terrestrials have been granted their own sections.

Each section has an introduction describing shared traits of the categorized flies: their construction, their usefulness on certain types of water during certain seasons, and the methods with which they may be most successfully fished. Please take note: purchase of this book will not automatically grant you fly fishing success. Fly fishing anywhere—especially in New Mexico—is much more than having the best flies in your box. And although we have provided some hints and suggestions about where and how to use each particular pattern, neither author is about to give away all their hard-won secrets. You may gain a few more clues through careful reading of *Fly Fishing in Northern New Mexico,* edited by Craig Martin (UNM Press, 1991).

There exist hundreds of good "introduction to fly tying" books and we have no wish to duplicate them. Our descriptions assume a basic familiarity with fundamental tying techniques like selecting the appropriate sizes of hackle for a particular hook size, handling and tying in common materials, and whip finishing. Unusual or especially important techniques for each fly will be described more thoroughly.

Fly fishing is fun. And so is fly tying. We hope we've produced not a labored text to be used as a reference for all time, but a celebration and suggestion of possibilities yet to be created. Explore!

Introduction to Dry Flies

More tomes have been written on tying and fishing dry flies than on any other segment of fly fishing. The goal in this section is to suggest some patterns peculiar to this part of the country: floaters that you can fish with full-time faith as to their effectiveness, jaunty joyriders of the riffles injected with the right juju to seduce any piscatorial prey. You see what happens when people talk about dry fly fishing!

When people speak sanely of dry flies they mean the airborne stage of an insect that has an aquatic nymph or larva. This includes stoneflies, caddisflies, mayflies, damselflies and midges. Some folks may also throw in terrestrial insects and even emergers caught in the water's film. It's fair to say that some part of the fly should be above the surface.

Rio Grande Cutthroat and Parachute Dry Fly

The real magic happens when the fish comes to the surface and takes a bit of floating fluff. The big snoot of a brown or cutthroat poking through the surface denies logic and Darwin and self-preservation. Even the fishes' refusals are thrilling! It is true that a good nymph pattern fished well will produce more and bigger fish, particularly on deeper streams, but Karen is content to devote at least a couple days every summer to small streams and dry flies for the simple thrill of hooking those eager little fish greedy for a small dry fly.

With the exception of a few early hatches (the Giant Stoneflies on the Pecos and Jemez waters, and the caddisflies on the Rio Grande come to mind) and a few unusual winter days on the Rio, dry flies are best fished in New Mexico after the waters have cleared and come down from their high Spring flows until late Fall when the water temperatures have dropped and fish become torpid.

Dry flies are usually cast upstream and allowed to float back downstream on a dead drift. Drag—when the fly moves at a different speed than the water around it—is most obvious and problematic when fishing dry flies in this manner. Mayfly imitations which "speedboat" downstream are usually not so attractive to trout as those that behave more like the real bugs. Reach casts, mends, curve casts, "high-sticking" the rod to keep line off the water—these are all useful techniques to the dry fly fisher. But don't forget that some caddis skate or buzz across the water, and mayflies will often dap the water as they are laying their eggs. "Waking" a big dry fly in whitewater can sometimes bring up behemoths from the depths. Meanwhile, most of New Mexico's miles of fishing is contained in small streams, perfect for tight casts with dry flies.

Fore and Aft Midge
Ed Koch, Barrie Bush

Hook: Standard dry fly hook, sizes 18–24
Thread: Black 8/0
Hackle: Grizzly

1. Tie on the thread and wrap a single thread base back to the hook bend. Tie in a grizzly hackle by the butt, hackle fibers curved toward the hook eye (dry fly style). Move the thread forward marginally.

2. Take two or three tight turns of hackle. Anchor firmly, *but do not clip.* Wrap the thread forward ¾ of the shank over the hackle, covering it smoothly and completely.

3. Disengage the hackle from the thread and continue with the thread to the hook eye. You can use the thread to cover any fibers that have been trapped against the hook shank for a neater appearance. Take an additional two or three turns of hackle as before, then tie off and clip excess. Whip finish.

If not for the size, this would be one of the easiest flies to tie. Also described as a "midge cluster" fly, this simple little pattern seems to give the same impression that mating midges provide as they congregate in little rafts on the water's surface, just as a Griffith's Gnat does. In the smallest sizes, though, it's much easier to tie than the standard Griffith's Gnat. It is difficult to see, even on the glassy water where midges are found; trail it behind a slightly larger dry fly for better perception.

Hare's Ear Trude

Bert and Marie Tallant

Hook: Standard dry fly hook, size 12–16
Thread: Brown 6/0
Ribbing: Fine gold wire or tinsel
Dubbing: Natural hare's mask or blend
Wing: Natural deer hair
Hackle: Grizzly

1. Tie on the thread and wrap back to the hook bend. Tie in the gold wire.

2. Dub a tapered body forward ⅔ of the hook shank; rib with the gold wire, then anchor the wire and clip excess.

3. Select a very small bunch of deer hair, stack the tips, and tie in as a down wing ⅓ shank length from the hook eye. Clip and overwrap the hair butts to form a base.

4. Tie in a grizzly hackle butt "dry fly style" with the hackle fibers curving toward the hook eye. Take three or four turns of hackle, tie off, then clip excess.

5. Whip finish a small head.

Bert and Marie report that this is one of their favorite choices for bright summer days—the fly may represent a grasshopper, an adult stonefly, or the ubiquitous caddisflies. The deer hair wing gives better buoyancy and a more natural appearance to the fly than the more common white calftail trude wing; dark elk hair may also be substituted. Be sure to use less hair rather than more for the wing. This will tie in firmly with less bulk, trap less water between the fibers when fished, and still give the appropriate down-wing appearance.

Bounce this fly through riffles (it floats high and well) or pop it up against meadow banks like a grasshopper.

Little Brown Fly

Karen Denison

Hook: Standard dry fly hook, size 14–18
Thread: Brown 6/0
Tail: Natural light elk
Body: Fine reddish brown poly or silk
Wing: Cream polypropylene yarn
Hackle: Brown

1. Mount the hook in the vise. Tie on the thread and wrap back to the standard dry fly wing position ¼ to ⅓ shank length from the hook eye. Separate the poly yarn to half the thickness of the finished wing. Anchor the poly yarn on the hook shank with a couple of tight wraps, then pull both ends upward. Wrap around the base of the post two or three turns as for a parachute-style wing. Clip the excess yarn to leave a finished wing post.

2. Move the thread to the hook bend. Select and stack 5 to 7 elk hairs, then tie in as a tail in a single bunch. Clip the hair butts so they will just reach the wing post.

3. Wrap a very small amount of dubbing around the tying thread and dub a slim, smooth body to cover the elk hair butts to the base of the wing.

4. Select a stiff-fibered hackle and tie in dry fly style behind the wing (with the dull side toward the hook eye, fibers curving forward). Add a tiny bit of dubbing to the thread and dub forward to just behind the hook eye.

5. Wrap two to three turns of hackle behind the wing post, then three turns just in front of the wing. Tie off and clip excess.

6. Whip finish.

This fly is simple, durable, and very attractive to trout. The fly's cream-colored poly wing tied as a single clump and the elk hair tail make it easy to see on the water, and the tinge of wing color helps distinguish it from foam. Folding the poly for the wing eliminates any excess tying bulk and keeps the body profile very slender. A size 16 LBF has often been successful in sunny runs where a brighter dry fly like an Elk Hair Caddis or Coachman Wulff is refused.

Karen likes this pattern best as a traditionally hackled fly to stand up on riffled water, but it also works well as a parachute pattern. Karen's husband Terry swears by this pattern and has been known to tie one onto his leader in the spring and replace it only when lost—with another Little Brown Fly.

Pott's Variation
Bruce Bliss

Hook: Standard dry fly hook, size 12–20
Thread: Black 6/0
Abdomen: DMC embroidery floss, yellow #726
Ribbing: Medium gold wire or flat tinsel
Wing: Deer hair
Shellback: Peacock herl

1. Tie on the thread and wrap a thread base back to the hook bend. Tie in three or four strands of peacock herl, the gold wire, and one strand of floss. Move the thread forward ⅔ of the hook shank.

2. Evenly wrap the floss forward, tie off and clip excess. Follow with the gold wire, tie off and clip.

3. Twist the herl several times to form a loose chenille. Fold forward, anchor firmly with the thread, and clip excess.

4. Clean and stack a small bunch of deer hair for the wing. Tie in with the tips just reaching the hook bend as you would an Elk Hair Caddis wing. Clip the hair butts and whip finish.

Fly patterns developed by Franz Pott are popular in Montana, where Bruce and Barbara have summered for many years. Bruce is a native Montanan, but has successfully used his variant pattern in local waters for a number of years. The standard Elk Hair Caddis is one of Karen's favorite commercially available flies, but the no-hackle yellow body and darker deer hair wing of this fly seem to make it more acceptable to New Mexico summer trout gone fussy. Give it a try, especially where there are the small yellow stoneflies called "yellow Sallies". Bruce notes that pyrite or fools' gold in many streams is incorporated into caddis casings, making them sparkle; he believes the gold tinsel in this imitation should be just as prominent.

Foam Stone
Richard Wilder

Hook: Any 2X or 3X long dry fly hook, size 6
Thread: Brown 3/0
Tail: Brown goose biots
Body: Orange closed-cell foam strip, ⅛ inch thick, 3/16 inch
    wide
Wing: Two mallard flank feathers coated with flexible
    cement
Hackle: Brown
Antennae: Brown rubber leg, fine

1. The most tedious part of this pattern is preparing the
wings, so prepare a number of feathers at one time. As messy
as it is, the most durable wings are made by dipping the
feathers one at a time in cement (like Dave's Flexament), then
pulling them through your fingers from butt to tip several
times to yield narrow, well-coated feathers. If you are careful,
you can stick the feather butts into a florist's green styrofoam

block (easily penetrated foam, but very dense) to dry. The feather tips may be trimmed to a rounded shape when completely dry.

2. Tie on the thread and lay down a thread base to the hook bend. Tie in two goose biots, one on each side, to form a short, forked tail.

3. Tie in the foam strip as you would a piece of chenille yarn. Move the thread forward to ¼ shank length from the eye of the hook. Wrap the foam forward with a slight overlap between wraps and stretch the foam for the correct body shape. Tie off and clip excess.

4. Tie on a prepared mallard flank feather to yield a wing that lies flat over the body and extends to just beyond the tail. Wings which are too long or too wide may cause the fly to land on the water upside down. Clip off the excess stem. Tie in the second prepared feather on top of the first but offset it slightly to give the impression of two overlapping wings.

5. Tie in two rubber antennae, projecting over the hook eye by ½ shank length.

6. Tie in the hackle by the butt, with the curve of the fibers toward the hook eye. Move the thread forward slightly, then take four or five turns of hackle. Some of the turns may be over the foam. Anchor the hackle and trim excess. Whip finish a large head.

7. Remove the fly from the vise and trim a broad "V" in the underside hackle to yield a very low-riding, yet unsinkable fly.

The Giant Stonefly adult of the Pecos and other northern watersheds is dark brown with bright orange underneath and at the leg junctions. When adult stoneflies are on the water, even small fish get greedy. We've seen little "doinkers" chase and peck repeatedly at a stonefly until it finally flies away or gets dragged under. The standard heavily hackled patterns for adult stoneflies seem intended to imitate these active, fluttering insects, but don't very well mimic the profile of a quiet adult. When fish are being selective (as can happen toward the middle or end of a hatch), this low profile version may be more readily taken. Despite its large size, it may take practice to see this fly on the water.

Rich has experimented over the years with variations of this pattern, which was influenced by Eric Leiser and Robert Boyle's K's Butt Salmonfly pattern. He likes the natural appearance of the feather wing, but admits that some of the synthetic winging materials might make acceptable substitutes. He also suggests a "more rubber" version: use short pieces of brown rubber leg for the tail, and substitute for the hackle two rubber legs tied in "Madam X" style.

Egg-Laying Caddis

Don Puterbaugh

Hook: Standard dry fly hook, size 14–18
Thread: Black 6/0
Egg-sack: Bright olive or chartreuse dubbing
Body: Black dubbing
Wing: Light elk body hair
Hackle: Furnace

1. Attach the thread and wrap a thread base back to the bend of the hook. Dub a medium-sized (larger than the diameter of the body) egg-sack just ahead of the bend. Dub a narrower black body forward toward the eye, covering ⅔ of the hook shank but leaving plenty of room for wing and hackle and head.

2. Clean and stack a small bundle of light or bleached elk hair. Position and anchor the wing so the hair tips extend to the bend of the hook. Angle-cut the butt ends and secure them well with thread.

3. Attach a furnace hackle dry fly style (fibers curving toward the hook eye) and cover up the thread base of the wing with hackle. Leave a little room just behind the eye for a small head. Whip finish.

Bill and two friends went up to the Arkansas River near Salida one May to fish the Mother's Day caddis hatch. While getting their licenses in the Arkansas River Fly Shop, the phone rang and the conversation went something like this:

> "I'm out here on the river just below Salida. The fish are popping all over the place and I can't catch a damn thing!"
>
> "Have you got any of those caddis with the green egg sack?"
>
> "No."
>
> "Well, we've still got a few dozen left. Maybe you ought to come in and get a few."

If he had his cell phone on the river, it's likely this angler had some additional problems besides the lack of the right fly pattern. This is the dry caddis of choice for the spring caddis hatches in southern Colorado and New Mexico and outfishes standard elk hair and peacock patterns. The fly works better as the egg-sack discombobulates and drags down in the water, so don't worry about dubbing too tightly. When dressing the fly with floatant, just put it on the wings and hackle.

Ginger Dun
Van Beacham

Hook: Standard dry fly hook, size 18–16
Thread: Ginger or tan, 6/0
Tail: Tan elk
Body: Ginger dun (Hareline #43)
Wing: Tan elk
Hackle: Ginger

1. Tie on the thread behind the eye and wrap a thread base to mid-shank. Select a small bunch of elk hairs, cleaned of underfur and tips evened. Tie in with the tips facing forward, then use the thread to stand them upright and divide them into two wings, Wulff-style. Trim off the hair butts and wrap the thread back to the hook bend, covering the hair butts smoothly.

2. Tie in a tail of similarly cleaned and stacked elk hair. Trim the hair butts to result in an even thickness from the base of the

tail to the base of the wing. This will make the abdomen seem smooth in appearance without the need for uneven dubbing along the length of the abdomen.

3. Use a small amount of the ginger fur to dub a slender body forward, ending just behind the base of the wing.

4. Tie in one ginger hackle, dry fly style.

5. Add a fraction more dubbing to the thread and move it forward of the wing, forming a front taper to the thorax and bolstering the wings into the correct position.

6. Wrap two or three turns of hackle behind and in front of the wing. Tie off, then clip excess. Whip finish a small head.

This is a straightforward hair-winged dry fly pattern, exceptional for its very particular color and local effectiveness. There is a mayfly which is present as an afternoon or evening hatch on many Sangre de Cristo streams from Santa Fe northward to the state line, from late June to mid-August; this pattern is its perfect imitation. The standard hackling and elk hair make it rugged and permit it to stand out to the eye when fishing ruffled water; on quiet water, a clipped bottom hackle, or a parachute version may be the ticket for more discriminating fish.

Guide and lifelong resident Van Beacham considers this an indispensable local dry fly.

Black Parachute
Al Troth, Nic Medley

Hook: Standard dry fly hook, size 10–20
Thread: Black 6/0 or 8/0
Post: White polypropylene yarn
Tail: Moose or elk hock
Body: Black dubbing
Hackle: Grizzly

1. Attach thread directly behind the eye and wrap back ⅓ of the way toward the hook bend.

2. Separate a strand of poly yarn to half the appropriate thickness for the wing you are tying—for a size 14 fly, this would be from fifteen to twenty poly fibers. Cut the strands into 1½" bundles. Attach the bundle in the middle, then pull both ends upward, wrapping up around the doubled poly then back down to form a secure wing post. Whip finish. Using a bodkin, apply a small amount of super glue to the thread wraps, keeping the glue out of the poly as much as possible. Stick the

hook with the prepared post into some cork or something to dry and make at least eleven more!

3. When completely dry, take one of the hooks with a prepared post and insert it back into the vise. Attach the thread behind the post and wrap back to the bend. Wrap a tiny ball of dubbing at the hook bend.

4. Cut about ten to twelve moose hairs, remove the underfur, then stack in a hair stacker. Anchor the tail in place atop the hook shank, flaring the tail into a fan shape over the dubbing ball, then cut the hair butts so that they extend up just behind the post. Lock down the tail and "underbody" by wrapping the thread from the bend to the post and back to the bend.

5. Dub as slim a body as possible working from the bend of the hook to the post. Wrap a little dubbing in an "X" pattern around the post so that there is continuous dubbing from the bend to just in front of the post. Finish with the thread in front of the post.

6. Tie in a good dry fly hackle just in front of the post with the bottom (concave) side down. Wrap the hackle up then down the post filling in hackle to the desired thickness (Bill uses five to six turns). Tying off parachute hackle without tying down a big wad of hackle fibers takes a little practice. With the thumb and index of your off hand, lift the hackle fibers up and away from the dangling thread and press the hackle stem against the base of the post. Bring the waiting thread up with your dominant hand and tie the hackle stem down just in front of the post. Snip off excess hackle.

7. Using the pinch and lift technique to get the hackle out of the way, dub the front third of the body up to just behind the eye. Whip finish.

8. Complete the fly by trimming the poly wing at an angle, the top of the post sloping down toward the tail to form a "natural" silhouette.

About twenty years ago, Al Troth was tying a version of this fly for the "gulpers" on Hebgen Lake. This version of the parachute comes via Nic Medley of Santa Fe. It consistently catches fish all over the country, even in the midst of other hatches. Bill's father caught a 20" brown on a size 12 Black Parachute during the midst of a heavy size 22 blue wing olive hatch. It was the only dry fly in the box. It consistently catches fish on all the freestone creeks of New Mexico, Wyoming, and Montana, though the white post can sometimes be hard to see on foamy water. Try black or orange for better visibility. Ninety-five percent of the time it lands rightside up on the water, unlike traditional or "upside-down" dries. All Bill's mayfly imitations are parachutes, but then he only uses dry flies as a last resort.

Magnet
Clayton Lewis

Hook: 3X long, curved shank, straight eye "Stimulator"
hook, sizes 10–16
Thread: Black or tan 6/0
Tail: Woodchuck hair or mixed brown and grizzly hackle
fibers
Ribbing: Fine gold or copper wire
Body: Natural hare's ear
Parachute wing: White or gold calftail
Lateral wings: grizzly hackle tips
Hackle: Brown and grizzly

1. Tie on the thread and form a thread base ⅓ shank length
from the hook eye. Tie in a small clump of calftail for the
parachute wing, wrapping the thread around the hook shank
on both sides of the hair to stand it upright. Carefully wrap
around the hair itself to form a strong post and a base for the
hackle.

2. Wrap the thread back to the hook bend. Spin a small bead of thread at the bend, then tie in the tail over the bead to flare the fibers. The tail should be as long as the hook shank. Tie in the ribbing.

3. Dub a body forward to the wing. Rib with the wire, then secure and clip excess. Use a bodkin to pick out some of the fur to make a fuzzier body.

4. Just in front of the wing, tie in on each side one grizzly hackle tip about as long as the hook shank, shiny side up. Use the thread to angle each wing about 45 degrees from the shank, but within the plane of the body.

5. Tie in and wrap one grizzly and one brown hackle parachute style. Secure and clip excess.

6. Whip finish a small head.

It's an Adams! It's a stonefly! We don't know what this interesting thing is, but it sure catches fish. Perhaps because it rides low in the water like the real bug, this fly seems to take more fish during stonefly hatches than traditional stonefly dries.

Getting the lateral wings to lie evenly takes a bit of practice. Choose narrow stiff-fibered hackle tips without too much "curve" to the stem.

Badger Variant
Jack Samson

Hook: Standard dry fly hook, size 10–14
Thread: Black 6/0
Tail: Golden badger hackle fibers
Body: Black floss
Rib: Gray 3/0 thread
Wings: Natural duck quill
Hackle: Golden badger, oversized by approximately
    two sizes

1. Attach thread just behind the eye and wrap back about ¼ of
the way down the shank. Cut two segments from a pair of duck
primaries (about ³⁄₁₆" long) and position them convex against
convex. Tie them in with the tips out over the eye, then build up
the thread just in front of the tie-in point to prop them up
perpendicular to the shank. If they've twisted, you may need to
make a wrap or two between the wings to separate them evenly.

2. Cover up the butt ends of the wings and move the thread down to the bend. Tie in a bundle of hackle fibers for a tail. You will be able to form a smoother body if you cut the butt ends of the tail even with the butt ends of the wings.

3. Attach the gray rib right at the base of the tail, then move the tying thread to the center of the shank. Attach the floss at this point, then move the tying thread up just behind the wings. Wrap the floss up to the thread, back to the base of the tail, then back to the thread and tie off. This should produce a nicely tapered body.

4. Rib the body evenly up to the waiting thread and tie off behind the wings.

5. Attach a hackle behind the wings and move the thread in front of the wings. Fully hackle the fly, putting about the same number of wraps behind and in front of the wings. Tie off in front of the wings, form a neat head, and whip finish.

Jack loves this fly for skating around the boulders on the Rio Grande. It is very similar to the Whitcraft, another effective pattern. Timing is the key to dry fly fishing success on the Rio Grande; water temperature and clarity make all the difference between a sound skunking and a memorable experience.

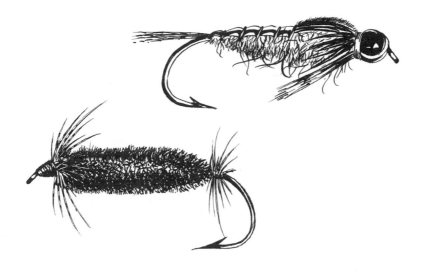

Introduction to Nymphs

While dry fly fishing has its charms and staunch supporters, you may have witnessed a good "nympher" pick fish after fish from pockets where no fish could be raised to a dry. It can be a successful approach. And there are frequent surprises to nymphing: will the next fish be a five-pound brown or a fifteen-pound carp? Often, you can't tell until the fish is in hand. Nymph fishing might best be described as: Mastering the Art of the Serendipitous Strike. Did the indicator pause fractionally or not? He who hesitates misses the fish. By the time you know the trout has the fly, the fish has already had the nymph too long.

In New Mexico, as in other parts of the country, the high water of spring runoff is a good time to put large, dark nymphs in front of the trout. You probably won't have much luck catching

Favorite (top) and Warden's Worry (bottom)

anything when the visibility is less than four inches, but the pre-runoff and post-runoff windows on freestone (undammed) rivers can be wonderful for big fish. Even during low water, a nymph will usually outfish a dry fly if it is properly presented without too large a splash. At times, nymphs can be too effective. No doubt that's why on some of Britain's holiest waters fly fishers are restricted to using dry flies for rising fish.

Nymphs are highly versatile. They can be fished in the film, chucked straight upstream, quartered upstream, lifted up like an emerging caddis, danced in the current like a streamer, and stack-mended straight downstream through the braids. There's no end of possibilities.

The flies described in this section are true nymphs; they imitate the nymphal form (some more impressionistically than others) of aquatic insects present in New Mexico waters. These naturals are available to trout as a food source all year, and may be the only insect form available to fish through the winter months. Trout are accustomed to them. Maybe that's why they work so well.

Most insect nymphs living in moving water are attached or cling to the river bottom. When dislodged, they tumble downstream along the bottom. You will note that most of the patterns in this section are weighted either with heavy wire or beads, or both. If you tie unweighted nymphs or are fishing small patterns in deep water, you may need to use split shot when fishing, although we much prefer to cast a weighted nymph. When wire is indicated, either lead or nontoxic wire may be used.

When fished appropriately deep, nymph flies bump against the bottom, hang up on rocks, get snagged and (hopefully) unsnagged, and are generally abused. Sometimes fish are even involved! Tying a robust fly and checking the hook periodically for sharpness is important. A hook hone may be useful for the serious nympher.

Strike indicators are a very personal matter. Variations on the theme are diverse, but detecting strikes without an indicator is extremely hard on most New Mexico streams when fishing slack line "dead drifts." Experiment until you find an indicator that you are comfortable seeing and casting.

Fishing nymphs can add new waters to your destination list and new seasons to your fishing year. And since you're bound to lose a few, aren't you glad you're a fly tyer?

Favorite
Chris Duffy

Hook: 2X long, heavy wire nymph hook, size 10
Bead: Medium gold
Weight: 12 turns, .025" wire
Thread: Tan 6/0
Tail: Bronze mallard flank fibers
Abdomen: Hare's ear dubbing
Rib: Fine copper wire
Shellback: Pearlescent mylar
Thorax: Hare's ear dubbing
Throat: Grouse breast feather
Wingcase and wings: Pheasant tail fibers

1. Thread the bead on the hook. Wrap a single layer of twelve turns of wire on the hook and push it forward inside the hole of the bead to center it on the shank. Spread a drop of superglue over the wire wraps to the bead. For production tying, Bill usually prepares several dozen flies to this stage.

2. Attach the thread behind the bead and tie in a small bundle of grouse fibers under the hook shank for a throat. Tie them in backwards, tips toward eye.

3. Wrap the thread back toward the bend of the hook over the wire and onto the shank. Attach the copper rib to the hook shank at the base of the wire wraps and wrap over it back to the bend.

4. Attach the tail and shellback at the bend.

5. Dub the abdomen up to the beginning of the wire wraps.

6. Pull the shellback over and tie off at same point. Rib with the copper wire.

7. Attach a bundle of pheasant tail fibers for the wingcase and emerging wings. Before folding, the tips of the pheasant fibers should reach the tips of the tail.

8. Dub the thorax forward to the bead.

9. Pull the wingcase over and tie down with 4 wraps of thread, then split the fibers equally to each side. Fold the pheasant tail fibers and the grouse throat back toward the bend. Wrap over the folds to form the emerging wings and throat, locking everything in.

10. Whip finish directly behind the bead.

Chris ties these Favorites by the gross for his fishing partner, Jody Feyas. They zoom all over northern New Mexico and southern Colorado "conditioning" the trout to this fly, but it continues to be an effective pattern. When Chris first described it to Bill over the phone, Bill got it wrong, of course, and came up with yet another Hare's Ear variation he now calls the Aviary. It has no shellback, a gold rib, and a peacock herl thorax. Bill likes Chris's version better.

In the larger sizes, #10 to #6, it has proven more effective than the standard Hare's Ear for both browns and rainbows. It is an excellent choice when the water is slightly off-color. Frequently, the fish will take the fly on the swing as it rises up through the current. While fishing in the Fall of 1997, Bill set his rod down briefly to scramble over a boulder and an 18" rainbow hit the Favorite while it was just hanging in the downstream current. He landed the fish! With all its flash, perhaps the "nymph" was mistaken for a small minnow. Don't lift the fly from the water too quickly.

Warden's Worry
(AKA Double Hackle Peacock or Depleted Uranium)
A. L. Cupp, Taylor Streit

Hook: 2X long, heavy wire nymph hook, size 6
Thread: Black 3/0 monocord
Weight: .035" wire
Rear hackle: Brown, undersized by two sizes
Body: Peacock herl
Front hackle: Grizzly, undersized by two sizes

1. Wrap fourteen turns of wire in a single layer over the central two-thirds of the shank. Apply a coating of superglue over the wire.

2. Attach the thread behind the wire and wrap back to the bend of the hook. Tie in a brown hackle by the butt with the shiny (top) side facing the eye of the hook, using at least six wraps of thread. It is easiest to have the feather tip trailing away from you on the far side of the hook.

3. Move the thread forward with a few widely spaced wraps to get it out of the way. Wrap three turns of hackle right at the hook bend, leaving at least ¹⁄₁₆" gap between the hackle and the wire turns. Anchor the last hackle turn, then move the thread back through the hackle, taking three or four turns to discourage the hackle from slipping off the bend. Return the thread to the front of the hackle turns. Clip off the excess feather.

4. Select ten strands of peacock herl and handle as a single bundle. For a size 6 hook, choose herl about seven inches long. Even the tips of the peacock bundle, then tie in the tips directly in front of the brown hackle. A loop of thread will be used to make a dubbing loop of the peacock forming a strong, tight chenille of herl and thread. Here's the easy way to proceed:

After tying in the peacock bundle, extend the thread down to the butt ends of the herl. Use a spring-retractor hackle plier (the inexpensive kind with a little wire hook on the end) to grasp both the bundle and the thread; this will be your dubbing loop tool. Fold the thread around your index finger to keep the bundle straight while you pull off thread to form a loop. Using your finger will ensure a little "slack" in the back of the loop and prevent herl breakage through overtightening of the loop. Take a couple of turns of thread around the hook shank at the loop tie-in to keep both ends of the loop close together, then move the thread forward to the front of the wire.

5. Twist the hackle pliers to form the chenille. Spin the loop in a counterclockwise direction when viewed from above; if you are wrapping all your materials over the hook shank and away from you, twisting the dubbing loop in this direction will yield a tighter, more durable chenille. Wrap the chenille around the shank forward to the waiting thread. Tie off firmly and remove the excess loop.

? dubbing spinner ?

40

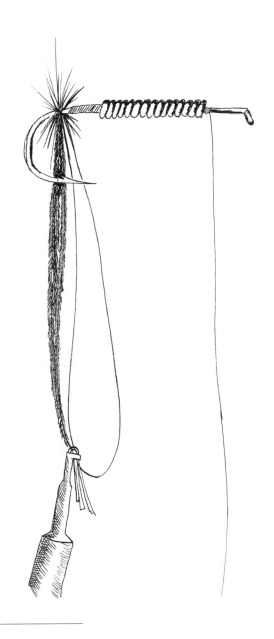

Step 4

6. Attach a grizzly hackle as before and wrap two or three turns. Tie off and remove excess.

7. Form a small thread head, then whip finish.

These are quite detailed instructions for a fly that can be tied more simply. Leaving out the loop, for example, will not affect the fly's ability to attract fish, but it will affect its durability. Yes, normally the fly ends up on a rock or in a tree before it can unravel, but there have been some wondrous days when we've caught forty big fish on the same fly. Modify the hook size and hackle configuration to your own taste from size 16 to 2; Bill favors tying them on #6 hooks. Be sure to keep this a very plump fly— the anorexic versions don't work as well. Bill's experience has been that this is a "dead-drift" kind of nymph. Sometimes in bigger water, he fishes them two at a time to get down fast to where the lunkers live. After fishing out the tail of a run or pool, chuck the flies above the prime lie at the head of the pool, right into the whitewater leading into the pool. Mend the line microseconds before the lip of the pool, and WHAM comes Shamu, the killer brown trout!

Callibaetis Nymph
Jan Crawford

Hook: 2X long, heavy wire nymph hook, size 16
Thread: Gray 6/0
Tail: Natural gray turkey marabou
Abdomen: Natural gray marabou and thread
Wingcase: Medium holographic silver flashabou, 1 strand
Thorax: Natural gray turkey marabou

1. Mount the hook in the vise and attach the thread leaving about a 3" tag end. Wrap back to the hook bend and place the tag in the material holder.

2. Anchor a small bundle of marabou at the bend, using at least three turns of thread. The tips should project over the bend to form a short tail no longer than the shank length. You can pinch off the tips (which gives a more natural appearance than cutting) if they are too long. Lash down the butt ends

along the shank to form an underbody, cut off any excess fiber up near the eye, then return the thread to the hook bend.

3. Tie in about five marabou fibers by their tips at the base of the tail. Insert the butt ends of the fibers along with the thread "tag" into your hackle pliers and spin them around to form a marabou chenille. Move the tying thread midway up the hook shank.

4. Wrap the marabou chenille around the hook shank, up to the waiting thread, and take one or two wraps to temporarily secure the chenille.

5. Tie in the strip of holographic tinsel with the excess trailing over the bend. Move the tying thread up to just behind the hook eye.

6. Re-spin the marabou chenille if necessary, then wrap a fluffy thorax up to the thread. Tie off and clip excess.

7. Fold the tinsel over the thorax toward the eye and tie off.

8. Whip finish.

The silver movement of natural marabou well imitates the swimming *Callibaetis* mayfly nymph. Twisting the fragile marabou fibers with the tying thread is a simple way to give longer life to a well-chewed fly pattern. This pattern has proven itself over and over again in the playa lakes of Colorado and New Mexico. The obese trout of Spinney and Stone lakes love it. You just need to get it in front of the trout. That's the main riddle of lake fishing— finding the fish. Wind seems to stimulate fish to feed in open water. If it's calm, try twitching this fly very slowly under a dry or an indicator along the moss edges, and in the moss pockets.

Caddis Casin'

Willie D. Lambert

Hook: 2X long, heavy wire nymph hook, size 16–12
Thread: Black 6/0
Weight: .020" wire, 10 turns
Body: Turkey tail fibers
Rib: Thread
Head: Bright caddis green dubbing

1. Wrap ten turns of wire weight onto the shank of the hook leaving a small space between the beginning of the wire wraps and the hook eye.

2. Superglue the wire to the shank. Attach the thread to the shank leaving about 10" of thread extending off the bend. (Place in the material holder, if you have one.) Wrap back to the hook bend.

3. Using the thread on the bobbin, attach the tips of the turkey tail fibers at the bend. Twist the fibers with the tying thread,

then wrap the noodle forward over the wire weight and stop
⅛" from the hook eye. Separate the thread from the fibers, then
tie off and clip the excess fibers.

4. Remove the reserved thread from the material clip and
counter-wrap the thread over the turkey fibers (wrap the opposite
direction used for the fibers) and tie off ⅛" behind the eye.

5. Dub a bright green head.

6. Whip finish.

According to Willie, this fly came to him in a dream. Of course,
he promptly woke up, tied a dozen, and the rest is history. This
is the fly of choice to fish in the Rio Grande nymph/streamer
combo. The Rio Grande is full of caddis and the Caddis Casin'
does better than an adequate job of imitating several of the
species present.

   Willie also ties this fly in a brass beadhead version, and
sometimes adds a collar of black ostrich or crystal chenille with
partridge fiber legs. With all the options, you know this fly is
going to be good. (If you wish to add a bead, it must be slipped
on first. If you wish to add legs and a collar, attach them between
steps 5 and 6.)

Barrie's Nymph
Barrie Bush

Hook: 3X long, 2X heavy streamer hook, size 14–18
Thread: Brown 6/0
Bead: Taper-drilled ¾₂" gold
Weight: .010" or none
Legs: Bronze mallard flank
Tail: Bronze mallard flank
Rib: Fine oval gold tinsel
Body: Olive/brown dubbing

1. Insert the hook point into the smaller hole of the bead. Place the hook in the vise. On larger sizes, it may be useful to seat the bead with a half-dozen wraps of fine wire, which are pushed up into the bead. The wire can be attached to the shank with superglue or thread.

2. Attach the thread just behind the bead and tie in two small bundles of bronze mallard fibers, one on each side of the fly, with the tips pointing "forward" beyond the hook eye.

3. Attach the rib with the excess hanging beyond the bend of the hook and anchor firmly by wrapping over it back to the bend.

4. Attach a sparse bundle of bronze mallard fibers in the normal fashion for a tail.

5. Dub a sparse body up to the tie-in point for the "backwards" mallard fibers.

6. Rib the body up to the same point and tie off.

7. Apply a small amount of dubbing to the thread, then pull back both bundles of legs. Apply the dubbing over the mallard fibers, forcing the legs back toward the rear of the fly and locking them in securely. Whip finish.

8. For a beautiful "soft" head, set aside a tiny application of dubbing. Start a second whip finish, then apply dubbing to the thread being wrapped inside the whip finish triangle. The dubbing will hide any visible thread. Voilà!

Like the commercial A. P. nymphs, this is an excellent all-purpose nymph pattern. One summer of guiding on the Pecos required no other patterns, according to Barrie. He switched flies only to see what else might work! Most guide clients, whether they'd admit to it or not, are looking for a high number of hookups, so why fight against success? Barrie's nymph imitates a wide range of small, dark nymphs that inhabit New Mexico waters.

Phyllis Diller
Ian Hoffman

Hook: Scud-style hook, size 12–16
Bead: Tapered brass to match hook size
Weight: .015" wire
Thread: Tan 6/0
Dubbing: Caddis green crystal dubbing (dyed rabbit
   plus mylar)

1. Slip a bead on the hook with the small opening of the bead at the hook eye. Mount the hook in the vise. Wrap ten turns of wire over the hook shank, break off excess, then slide the wire wraps up into the bead as far as it will slide. This will help "center" the bead at the hook eye as well as give the fly a proportioned underbody. Apply a drop of superglue to the wire and let dry completely.

2. Attach the thread behind the bead and wrap over the wire to the hook bend. Twist dubbing around the thread and dub

forward to the bead forming a body that smoothly tapers from a small abdomen to a large thorax.

3. Whip finish behind the bead and clip thread. Pick out the dubbing to give a "messy" appearance.

If this fly looks like it just got out of bed on a bad-hair day, so much the better. The bright green color with mylar flashes makes a great fly for the colored water of Springtime. It has become one of Karen's standard early season Rio Grande flies used as an attractor with a more representative pattern behind it. It is less effective when the water clears. An even uglier and yet more durable fly can be made by applying the dubbing in a loop. Occasionally, chenille yarn of the right color can be found.

According to Ian, this pattern was developed for parts north by Pete Cardinal, a guide on the Missouri River in Montana. It is described here because it is not a commercially available pattern, nor one that is widely known around here. It has proved perfect for some of our rougher watersheds.

Coachman Special

Karen Denison

Hook: Standard nymph hook, size 12–18
Thread: Tan 6/0
Weight: .015" wire
Tail: Hare's mask or coastal deer body hair
Abdomen: Red single-strand floss
Thorax: Peacock herl
Hackle: Grizzly

1. Mount the hook in the vise. Starting at mid-shank, wrap forward ten turns of wire, then wrap three turns back over the first layer at the thorax to form an underbody. Allow ample space between the wire wraps and the hook eye for the collar. Apply a drop of superglue to the wire and let dry completely.

2. Attach the thread and wrap over the wire to form a thread base. Move the thread to the hook bend.

3. Tie in a small, short tail of soft hair, allowing the hair butts to be used as an underbody that just meets the wire wraps. Clip off excess hair.

4. Tie in a piece of single-strand floss. Move the tying thread forward to the back of the thorax. Tightly spiral the floss forward to completely cover the underlying hair and a bit of the wire, making a slender abdomen. Tie off with the waiting thread and clip excess.

5. By the tips, tie in two or three peacock herls. Twist the herl around the tying thread to form a reinforced chenille, then wrap the chenille forward to completely cover the wire thorax. Take care not to let the chenille prematurely slip forward off the wire. Finish in front of the wire, disengage the thread from the herl, and tie off. Clip excess herl.

6. Tie in a grizzly hackle by the butt with the fibers curving back toward the bend (streamer style). Make one or two wraps, anchor the stem, and clip excess. Wrap back over the fiber butts to form a collar, then whip finish and clip thread.

Peacock herl and red floss—how can you beat this combination? The long, slender abdomen turns darker in the water, but retains its smooth sheen. Karen has fished this pattern for ten years and it is wonderful for high-country waters and appears especially attractive for cutthroats. (For unknown reasons, it has also produced strikes from fussy New Zealand brown trout who were refusing Pheasant Tails and other similar patterns.) Dead drift the pattern as you would a Hare's Ear or Prince nymph.

Yellowbelly
Dirk Kortz

Hook: 3X long, curved shank, straight eye "Stimulator"
    hook, size 8
Thread: Red 3/0
Tail: Deer body hair
Rib: Medium gold tinsel
Abdomen: Dark hare's ear and antron blend
Thorax: Dark gray synthetic
Belly: Medium yellow chenille
Legs: Deer body hair
Head: Thread

1. Mount the hook in the vise, tie on thread and spiral back to the hook bend.

2. Tie in a tail of deer hair about half the length of the hook shank. Tie in a piece of gold tinsel for ribbing. (Bill prefers to keep his ribbing on a spool mounted in a floss bobbin; you

can apply more tension, control the wraps better, and waste less tinsel.)

3. Dub forward a tapered body of dark hare's ear extending ⅔ the length of the hook. Spiral the ribbing forward through the dubbing and tie off.

4. Tie in two one-inch strips of yellow chenille on the underside of the body with the excess trailing back toward the hook bend. Tightly dub and wrap a thorax of the gray synthetic material. Pull the chenille forward and tie off underneath and behind the head.

5. On the underside of the body (as if for a beard), tie in deer hair legs. Tie them long enough to reach the hook point.

6. Wrap thread liberally to build a good-sized red head. Whip finish.

Although this fly is derived from a mayfly nymph imitation (the Gold-ribbed Hare's Ear), it more effectively imitates a stonefly nymph, a caddis pupa, or a forage fish—just about everything except a mayfly. Because the pattern imitates a variety of trout foods, Dirk ties it to alter on the stream. For simulating a golden or light brown stonefly nymph, shorten the legs, thin out the tail, then dead drift it in the current. For a rising caddis pupa, remove the tail and fish it down and across, raising it rapidly toward the surface at the end of the swing. As a forage fish imitation, it should be fished streamer fashion down and across, then retrieved upstream at various speeds, interspersed with pauses.

Although this is obviously a versatile pattern, Dirk still considers it a specialty item. It is not something he uses every time he goes out fishing, but when the time is right, it can be very effective. Dirk has had the most success with it on the Rio Chama and the Rio Grande—including the upper Rio Grande near South Fork, Colorado, where it has provided for some very exciting days.

This fly pattern has been around for a while and reports of its effectiveness continue to trickle in from some unlikely sources.

Woven Stone
Bill Orr

Hook: Dai-Riki 700-B or 4X long, heavy wire streamer
   hook with the shank bent slightly ⅓ shank length
   from the hook eye, size 12–2

Thread: Dark brown 3/0

Weight: Wire of appropriate size, for the thorax only

Antennae: Dark brown goose biots

Eyes: Black plastic bead chain or plastic dumbbells

Tail: Dark brown goose biots

Abdomen: Dark brown and cream New Dub (or ultra
   chenille for larger sizes) on spools loaded into floss
   bobbins

Thorax: Dark brown goat dubbing (Kaufman's blend is
   best)

Wingpads: Turkey tail treated with fixative or Flexament
   (See the Foam Stone pattern directions for treating the
   turkey tail feathers with Flexament in preparation for
   tying.)

NOTE: This fly is unnecessarily complicated and is best done in stages. Like some of Dave Whitlock's more realistic patterns, it seems to benefit from the judicious use of superglue.

1. Attach the thread directly behind the hook eye, then attach two goose biots for the antennae, one on each side, so that they flare out forward and away from the hook eye. Attach a pair of eyes just behind the biots, crisscrossing with the thread. Whip finish and superglue the wraps over the eyes. Set the hook in a cork board and allow the glue to dry completely.

2. Wrap about ⅔ of the thorax area with wire. Use needle-nosed pliers to flatten the wire wraps into a broader thorax and apply superglue. Set in a cork board to dry.

3. Attach the thread at the bend in the shank and wrap evenly back to the bend of the hook. For the tail, position one biot on each side of the hook and wrap forward over the butt ends of the biots all the way back to the bend in the shank, making an even underbody.

4. Tie in the tips of the New Dub right at the bend in the shank, keeping the dark color on one side of the shank and the light color on the other. Wrap tying thread over both strands to the base of the tail, then back to the bend in the shank; this will help anchor the chenille and also provide a flattened underbody. Whip finish and clip off the tying thread.

5. The trick to weaving is getting out of the "wrapping" mode. *Never* does either piece of New Dub go 360 degrees around the shank. The dark and the light material are "hooked" around each other at the 180 degree marks along the side of the abdomen. The dark stays on top and the light stays on the bottom. Weave the abdomen up to the bend in the shank.

Step 5. Have vise pointed away.
Don't switch hands. 1. Light (R)
goes under to left.

2. Dark hooks under light and goes
across top of shank.

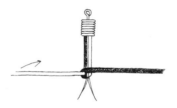

3. Light goes underneath.

4. Dark hooks under light and goes
across top of shank.

5. Light goes underneath.

58

Bill prefers to superglue the front end of the weave and cut the gluey material with an old pair of scissors. It will stay.

6. Reattach the tying thread at the rear of the weighted thorax and dub a thin layer of mohair forward over the glued part of the weave and a bit of the wire thorax.

7. The wingpads are made by taking a section of treated turkey tail, folding it in half, and then angle-cutting one end and blunt-cutting the other. When folded, the folded edge should be shorter than the "open" side. Unfold the wingpad and attach by the blunt-cut edge near the rear of the thorax, letting the inverse "V" project back toward the tail. Dub forward a bit. Cut and tie in a second wingpad. Dub. A third wingpad. Dub.

8. Whip finish just in front of the eyes.

Is it worth all the trouble? Probably not, but it looks really, really cool when you get it right, and it does catch fish. Many of the local non-catch-and-release fishermen like this fly as a "Hell-grammite" or dragonfly nymph imitation. It has also fooled some of the larger and more jaded browns in the public sections of the Pecos.

For folks looking for this and other weaves, check *The Art of Weaving Hair Hackle for Trout Flies* by George F. Grant (1971).

Little Yellow Stonefly Nymph
Tyce McLarty

Hook: Standard dry fly hook, size 16–14
Thread: White 6/0
Tail: Pheasant tail fibers
Rib: Olive thread or floss
Abdomen: Chartreuse green dubbing
Thorax: Chartreuse green dubbing and natural rabbit
    guard hairs
Wingcase: Peacock herl
Head: Thread

1. Wrap the hook shank with thread, then dub a small lump at the bend to split the tail. Tie in two or three pheasant tail fibers on each side of the hook. Tie in the ribbing material.

2. Dub the abdomen forward to just past the mid-point of the hook. Wind the rib forward and tie off. Tie in four to six peacock herls for the wingcase on top of the hook shank with the excess laying back toward the hook bend.

3. A dubbing loop is used to create a shaggy, yet secure thorax for the fly. Form a dubbing loop with the thread and twist the dubbing material on one side. Take a small bunch of rabbit guard hair, put it in the loop, and spread it evenly along the dubbing. Twist the loop, then wrap the thorax, spreading and folding the guard hairs toward the bend.

4. Fold the peacock herl wingcase forward and tie off. Wrap a small thread head and whip finish.

5. Trim the guard hairs from the bottom of the fly to create legs extending from the sides of the thorax.

Stoneflies of the genus *Isoperla* are common throughout the southern Rockies. Fish this pattern during a hatch of Little Yellow Stones, or as a searching pattern during Spring or early Summer. Although Tyce's original pattern does not include a weighted wire underbody, both Karen and Bill would choose to add at least ten wraps of 0.015" wire to the hook shank before anything else.

Poundmeister
Taylor Streit

Hook: Large-gap nymph hook, size 10–4
Thread: Gray 6/0
Underbody: Wool or wool yarn
Abdomen: Gray beaver or muskrat
Rib: Medium gold wire or pearl crystal flash
Hackle: Medium dun saddle
Shellback and thorax: peacock herl

1. Tie on thread behind the hook eye and lay down a single layer thread base. Return the thread to a position ⅓ shank distance behind the hook eye.

2. Use either wool dubbing or one small strand of wool yarn to build an even, chunky underbody back to the hook bend.

3. Tie in the gold wire and four to six strands of peacock herl by the tips.

4. Tie in the hackle feather "dry fly" style: by the hackle butt, with the curve of the fibers facing the eye of the hook.

5. Using the soft beaver or muskrat, dub forward to evenly cover the underbody.

6. Palmer the hackle forward in four to six turns to meet the waiting thread. Tie off and remove excess.

7. Fold the peacock herl bundle forward to form the shellback. Anchor securely with a couple of wraps, *but do not clip excess.*

8. Counter-wrap the gold wire to the front of the abdomen. This means that if you normally turn your thread and hackle over the hook shank and away from you, then wrap the wire in the opposite direction. It will crisscross the hackle stem on each turn (wiggle the wire a little as you turn it to avoid pinching down the fibers) and reinforce the construction. Tie off the wire and trim.

9. Grasp the peacock herl butts together with the thread and twist to form a chenille. Wrap from the front of the abdomen to just behind the hook eye to form a sloping head and thorax. Disengage the herl from the thread and tie off the herl. Clip excess.

10. Form a small whip finish head.

Taylor has been fly fishing forever and guides both locally and in Argentina. Old-timers will remember his store in Taos, and a newer endeavor is his recently published book, *Taylor Streit's No-Nonsense Guide to Fly Fishing in New Mexico*. This fly comes highly recommended by his fishing partner, Garrett VeneKlasen.

The Poundmeister was originally developed to imitate a cranefly larva, which is common on lower elevation streams. The real thing is very chunky, and so should be the imitation. The underbody could be made with almost anything, as long as it's inexpensive and easy to lay down. Avoid dubbings with stiff guard hairs unless you intend it to show though in places. Karen has gotten from a friend a little bag of raw wool that has served well for underbodies for several years. It's easy to twist for extra bulk or use flat for a smooth surface. Be sure to choose a hook with a gap sufficient to accommodate the bulky dressing and still effectively hook the fish. Taylor notes that a number of the popular long shank hook styles aren't very useful for this pattern.

Taylor ties this unweighted—except for the occasional addition of a gold bead—for maximum versatility while fishing. Our own bias would lead us to use a single layer of wire weight wrapped beneath the underbody to avoid requiring split shot.

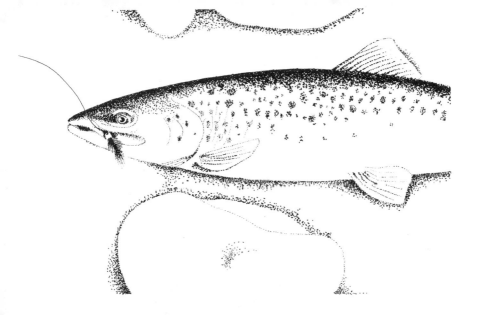

Introduction to Streamers

"Big fish, big fly" is an adage that holds some truth. Fish become fat by eating large meals such as other fish. Frequent exceptions to this rule are the famous tailwaters such as the San Juan, the Green, and the Bighorn. Those trout grow large on a continuous conveyor belt of tiny bugs.

The Rio Grande is New Mexico's prime streamer water. Yes, Rio Grande Reservoir way up there in Colorado does make the Rio a tailwater by technicality, but by the time it reaches us in New Mexico the river has been subjected to so many inflows and outflows that the equalizing effects of the dam cannot be felt. One theory about trout behavior is that trout that experience the wide fluctuations of sediment, temperature, and flow like they do on the Rio must become more opportunistic feeders. They do not have the opportunity to become conditioned to the continuous

Egg-sucking Leech

snacks coming down a tailwater conveyor belt. It's the T-bone steak versus the crudité theory. Wouldn't you choose the steak if it was going to be your only meal for awhile? Regardless, any fly fisher heading up to the Rio should have a box well stocked with Woolly Buggers, Egg-sucking Leeches, Soft Hackle Streamers, Bucktails, Matukas, and Crayfish.

Streamers as a group are usually meant to be actively moved under the surface of the water, often including marabou and other materials that pulsate and enhance the motion of the fly. The most frequent way to fish streamers is to quarter them upstream, then dodge them around holding structure as the fly drifts downstream. By mending, the cast can be extended to a reasonable length, but at some point the streamer is going to swing across current and end up directly downstream of the fly fisher. Fish strike at any point, including directly downstream! A big reason for the effectiveness of streamers may also be that they tend to be in the water longer per cast than other types of flies. Good streamer fishermen use a minimum of casting and a maximum of fishing the fly.

Guide Jarrett Sasser has an interesting setup for fishing a two-fly streamer/nymph combo. The streamer is dead-drifted along with the nymph for most of its route, then twitched and stripped at the end of the swing to tease up any suspicious fish that may have followed without striking. It's really a quadruple combo when you think about it—two very different kinds of flies fished in two ways on each cast.

Never overlook streamers for New Mexico lakes. You may want to add a sink-tip or full sink line to your gear to stretch your techniques a bit. At least nine species of fish have been fooled by the Egg-sucking Leech in Abiquiu Lake: kokanee salmon, brown trout, rainbow trout, walleye, smallmouth bass, white crappie, bream, channel catfish, and the wily carp—not a bad record for a fly that looks like nothing in particular.

Tie a bunch and expect to lose a few if you're fishing them close to the cover that hides big fish!

Brown and Yellow Bucktail
Scott Geary

Hook: 6X to 8X long streamer hook, size 8–2
Thread: Black monocord
Tag: Red monocord
Body: Medium flat gold tinsel
Underwing: Bright yellow bucktail
Overwing: Natural brown bucktail
Cheeks: Jungle cock or substitute (go ahead, try to track
    down the real thing!)
Head: Thread

1. Mount the hook in the vise and wrap a small bead of red monocord thread at the bend of the hook. Whip finish, trim the excess thread, and saturate with head cement.

2. Tie in black monocord thread near the eye of the hook. Tie in a long strand of gold tinsel at or near the eye of the hook. Wrap the tinsel back to the red tag, then forward to the eye of

the hook and tie off. Wrapping two layers assures a more smooth and durable tinsel body.

3. Select a small bunch of yellow bucktail and tie in securely on top of the hook shank at the head of the fly. When tied in, the bucktail should be only slightly longer than the hook. Tie in a small bunch of brown bucktail over the yellow. Clip the butt ends of the bucktail at an angle and wrap thread over the butt ends.

4. With thumb and forefinger, pull upward on the bucktail wing. Wrap several turns just behind the wing. This will set the wing at an angle that gives the fly a pulsating action in the water.

5. Tie in two jungle cock eyes along each side of the wing. Tie them in at the same angle as the wing. (The best substitute is the black and white tips of woodduck flanks, one from the right and left side of a feather, and coated with head cement.)

6. Whip finish.

The Brown and Yellow Bucktail was developed by Scott almost ten years ago for brown trout on the Rio Grande. It has proven itself many times since in other waters, too. It is a local "upgrade" on the standard Little Brown Trout Streamer, which doesn't have such blatant strike triggers. The high contrast between the brown and yellow, the gold flash down the entire body length, the good juju of jungle cock; it's more than any brown trout can stand.

It has caught fish dead-drifted, fished by standard streamer retrieve, and just hanging in the current. Wyoming's version of this fly is the Platte River Special, a featherwing variation of the key brown and yellow theme. Be sure and have a few Brown and Yellow Bucktails tied up by the time Fall rolls around.

Bug-Eyed Betty
Ed Adams, Dirk Kortz

Hook: 3X long streamer hook, size 6
Thread: Red monocord
Eyes: Extra large bead chain or large barbell
Tail: Equal parts brown and yellow marabou
Rib: Fine copper wire
Body: Brown and yellow variegated chenille (brindle)
Hackle: Grizzly

1. Attach the thread near the eye and wrap ¼ of the way back toward the hook bend. Build up a small valley of thread wraps at this point to rest the eyes in. Attach the eyes with both crisscross and figure-eight wraps to secure them to the shank. Whip finish and clip the thread. Cement the wraps with a drop of superglue and set aside to dry completely.

2. Reattach the tying thread behind the eyes, then tie in the copper wire rib. Wrap over the copper rib back to the bend of the hook and put the rib in the material holder. (It's easier to have the rib spooled on a bobbin.)

3. Attach a small bundle of brown marabou as a tail, then a small bundle of yellow marabou on top. The finished tail should be about one hook shank length beyond the hook bend. Adjust the length by pinching off excess marabou with your fingers for a natural appearance, rather than using scissors. Wrap over the butt ends toward the eyes, then back to the bend to form an even underbody. Expose about ³⁄₁₆" of the chenille core by stripping the fibers off with your thumbnail. Attach the chenille core at the hook bend.

4. Move the thread up just behind the eyes. With even wraps, wrap the chenille up to the waiting thread and tie off. Strip off the down from the base of a grizzly saddle hackle and attach it by the butt just behind the eyes. Ideally, the hackle should wrap on edge with the bright side or top toward the eyes and the fibers curved toward the tail.

5. Palmer wrap the hackle over the hook shank and away from you back to the waiting wire at the hook bend. Catch the hackle with the wire and wrap the wire rib over and away up to the waiting thread at the eyes. Wiggle the wire a little as you turn it to avoid catching hackle fibers underneath. (In contrast to counter-wrapping, moving materials up and down the hook shank in opposite directions achieves the same reinforcing but produces an even more durable fly that doesn't loosen previously tied-in materials.) Tie off the wire with the thread as you would any other rib. Wiggle the wire under the thread wraps to break it, thus saving your scissors.

6. Wrap some more thread around the eyes if you need to neaten things up a bit. A big, ugly head on this fly is a plus. Whip finish.

Dirk Kortz told us about this fly, but says the credit for its creation lies with Ed Adams up in Questa. This fly, like the previous bucktail, has the essential brown and yellow combination. Note that although it is tied with the hook mounted normally in the vise, the fly will ride hook point up in the water because of the bead chain eyes. It's proven most successful ticked and twitched along the bottom like a crawdad and fished in the classic down and across streamer fashion. Bill has tried adding rattles, propellors, and scent, but none of them seem to increase its effectiveness beyond its current maximum. It is one of those flies that will pull up a few fish when nothing else will.

Tinsel Tail
Homer Southerland

Hook: 2X-4X streamer hook, size 2–6
Thread: Brown 3/0
Tail: Mylar tinsel, green on one side, gold on reverse, or all
    gold
Body: Tinsel chenille, variegated brown/copper size
    medium or large
Hackle: Brown

1. Tie on thread and wrap back to the hook bend to form a
thread base. Build up a small thread "lump" at the bend.

2. Just in front of the thread "lump," tie in twenty strands of
mylar to form a ½" tail. (Five strands folded in half twice will
give the right amount.) Tie close to the thread lump to flare the
tail.

3. Wrap the thread forward and back over the shank to level it,
finishing at the tail.

4. Tie in the brown hackle by the butt, shiny (top) side facing away from the eye. Strip the chenille fibers from ¼" of the core thread, then tie in by the core. Move the tying thread forward.

5. Wrap the chenille forward and tie off at the eye. Palmer the hackle forward and tie off.

6. Form a small thread head and whip finish.

This fly, like others in the nymph and streamer sections, may be fattened up by laying down an underbody of wool or wool yarn tied flat. This is particularly useful for larger hook sizes. They may be weighted, although Homer fishes them unweighted with a sinking line.

This fly was developed specifically for Stone Lake, where it has been *the* fly for a couple of seasons. The size 6 is preferred early to late Summer, then larger sizes in the Fall. Who knows what the fish take it for—it's not a damselfly, and with its short, stiff tail it's not a typical streamer fly. But those who've had the fortune to try it know that large fish sure like it! Fish it as you would a damsel nymph pattern.

Egg-sucking Leech
Bill Orr

Hook: 3X long streamer hook, size 6
Weight: .035" wire, 14 turns
Thread: Black 3/0
Tail: Black marabou
Rib: Black Kevlar (on a bobbin)
Body: Black chenille
Hackle: Black saddle
Head: Steelhead orange glo-bug yarn

1. Mount the hook in the vise and wrap fourteen turns of wire on the middle ⅔ of the shank. Superglue the wire and let dry in a cork board. Make up at least a dozen weighted hooks.

2. Attach the tying thread just behind the wire and tie in the Kevlar rib. Wrap over the rib with the tying thread to the hook bend. Put the Kevlar in the material holder.

3. Attach a fluffy marabou tail and clip the butt ends so that they do not extend up onto the wire wraps. Use your thumbnail to pinch off the tail so that it is the same length as from the eye to the bend.

4. Use your thumbnail again to strip off the chenille fibers and expose a ¼" length of the thread core. Tie in the chenille by its exposed core. Move the thread up just in front of the wire, then wrap the chenille evenly up to the waiting thread and tie off.

5. Prepare a black saddle hackle by stripping off the fluff at the base and tie in the butt on edge, so that the top of the feather is toward the eye, the fibers curving back toward the tail, just in front of the wire wraps. Whip finish and clip off the tying thread. The Kevlar thread will now be used as both rib and thread.

6. Wrap the saddle hackle back to the waiting Kevlar, palmering it evenly over the body. At this point, let the Kevlar rib dangle below the hook and spin it clockwise to reduce its diameter. This will help it slip down through the hackle fibers.

7. Catch the hackle with the Kevlar and palmer the Kevlar from the base of the tail up to where the hackle was tied in, taking care to wiggle the thread through the hackle fibers so as not to trap any against the hook shank. (This overwrapping is the same trick employed in the Bug-Eyed Betty, which reinforces the hackle and will produce a truly bulletproof leech or Bugger.)

8. Cut off a one-inch piece of leech/egg yarn. Use the Kevlar to roll the egg yarn strand evenly around the hook shank near the eye. Take two more really tight turns with the Kevlar at the same location. Use your fingers to pull the egg yarn back

toward the rear of the fly, getting the thread exposed. Whip finish and clip the Kevlar.

9. Now stroke and pull all the yarn out over the eye and snip it off just in front of the eye. If you rolled it evenly around the hook shank, you will now have a perfect egg on the head of your Woolly Bugger.

Although this fly was invented in Alaska by combining the two most effective Alaska flies, the Woolly Bugger and the egg fly, it has really come into its own as a black and orange combination down here below the 49th parallel, or in our case, the 37th. If there is one all-species fly for New Mexico, this is it. Fish it in every way imaginable. Unweighted versions at night produce a nice wake and some big fish. Bill's New Mexico species count with this fly now stands at eleven. He needs to take it farther south to add some additional species!

Soft Hackle Streamer
Van Beacham

Hook: 2–3X long streamer hook, size 6
Thread: 6/0 to match marabou at the head
Weight: Small lead or large beadchain eyes, optional
Underbody: Gold tinsel
Body: Long fiber "spey style" marabou, such as from
    Wapsi
Lateral line: Crystal flash
Collar: Partridge breast feather
Fins: Paired "church window" pheasant breast feathers

1. Tie on thread behind the hook eye and lay down a small thread base. Anchor and figure-eight with the thread a pair of small lead eyes on top of the hook shank ⅛" behind the hook eye. Secure with a drop of superglue; allow to dry completely.

2. Wrap a thread base backward to the hook bend. Tie in the gold tinsel. Move the thread forward to mid-shank. Wrap overlapping spirals of the tinsel forward to the thread, tie off and clip excess tinsel.

3. Select a marabou feather with long fibers and a very limber stem. Fold the feather in half lengthwise by stroking the fibers together from both sides of the stem. Tie in the tip of the stem, with the folded feather fibers pointing toward the hook bend.

4. Move the thread forward about ½" (⅙ shank length). Carefully wrap the marabou forward to the thread while keeping the fibers folded toward the hook bend. Anchor the marabou stem and clip off excess feather.

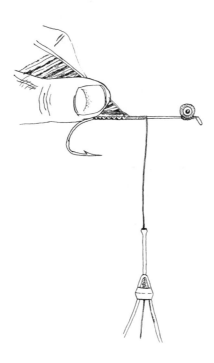

Step 4. Tie in by tip. Fold marabou back as you wrap it.

5. Tie in a second marabou feather as before, and wrap forward an equal distance before securing and removing excess. Repeat the process with a third marabou feather, ending ¼ to ½" behind the lead eyes.

6. Select eight strands of crystal flash. Tie in four strands on each side of the body, reaching beyond the hook bend to the full length of the marabou fiber body.

7. Tie in a grouse or partridge breast feather by the butt, fibers curving back over the body and wrap several turns to form a collar. Clip excess.

8. Select two pheasant breast feathers exhibiting strong, short, curved stems. Tie one along each side by the butt with the feather tip curving out from the body of the fly. Wrap over the feather butts and around the lead eyes; whip finish a smooth head.

This fly in the water is a thing of undulating beauty. Van prefers one of three body color combinations, from head to tail: brown/white/black, black/brown/black, and brown/yellow/white. The latter may be especially useful during the Fall. Single colors brown or black are okay, but don't seem quite as effective.

The folded marabou trick comes from the folded hackle technique used to tie Atlantic salmon flies. It results in all of the fibers projecting backward and laying naturally along the body instead of sticking out at right angles to the shank in a giant puffball. Puffballs probably catch fish, but if you can master this trick your flies will be full bodied without the "bad hair" look.

Homer's Damsel Nymph
Homer Southerland

Hook: Mustad 87160 (English bait hook) or 4X long
    streamer hook, sizes 8–10
Thread: Olive 6/0
Tail: Dark olive marabou
Body: Large olive larva lace with gold crystal flash inserted
Dubbing: Olive fur blend or dark olive marabou
Wingcase: Tan raffia or swiss straw
Eyes: Large gold bead chain

1. Mount the hook in the vise and attach tying thread. Wrap a
small thread base, then figure-eight on the beadchain eyes.
Whip finish behind the eyes, clip thread, and place the hook in
a production board. Apply superglue. Allow to dry completely.

2. When glue has dried, remount the hook in the vise and
attach the thread behind the eyes. Wrap a thread base to the
hook bend. Tie in a clump of marabou for the tail.

3. Prepare the larva lace for the body by threading one strand of gold crystal flash through the center of the lace. Trim the tie-in end at an angle, and anchor to the hook shank with the cut side against the hook.

4. Dub forward sparsely over the marabou butts to yield an even underbody, stopping ¼ hook shank from the hook eye. Wrap and twist the larva lace to form a flat abdomen, taking care not to overlap the turns. Meet the waiting thread, anchor, and clip excess.

5. Tie in the raffia wing case with the excess pointed toward the tail. Apply dubbing to the thread or tie in marabou by the tips and twist around the thread. Dub forward all around the bead chain with figure-eights, ending between the beadchain and the hook eye.

6. Pull the wingcase forward and anchor; clip excess. Whip finish.

From the gentleman who brought us the Tinsel Tail comes another useful variation on a damsel nymph. The gold flash inside the body lace is a nice touch and not so hard to produce with the large diameter tubing. Homer sometimes also uses gold/olive tinsel in the tail.

The hook choice is subject to taste: the strong curve of the English bait hook may cause the fly to twist in the water when retrieved, but the more typical straight-shanked streamer hook also produces a very effective fly.

Holographic Matuka
Jarrett Sasser

Hook: 3X to 6X straight eye streamer hook, size 8–4

Thread: Olive 6/0

Eyes: Spirit River paste-on holographic, placed onto gold barbell

Weight: .030" wire

Rib: Fine gold or copper wire

Wing: Natural rabbit zonker strip overdyed olive

Body: Olive dubbing

Lateral line: Holographic tinsel

Throat: Grizzly dyed orange hackle fibers

1. Tie in the thread and attach the barbell eyes approximately ¼" from the hook eye using a crisscross and figure-eight wrap. Whip finish and clip thread. Wrap wire weight in a single layer from the eyes nearly to (but ⅛" from) the hook bend. Apply superglue to the wire weight and eyes and set aside to dry. Make up at least a dozen.

2. When dried, remount the hook in the vise and reattach thread. Attach the rib securely between the weight and the bend of the hook. Wrap over it right to the bend. Dub an olive body forward just over the barbells, crossing around the barbells to cover up any thread wraps.

3. Flip the hook over in the vise to finish the fly. Cut a rabbit strip so that it is just slightly shorter than the hook shank. Attach it with the tying thread just in front of the barbells on the opposite side of the hook shank so the hairs lay toward the hook bend. Using the wire rib at the hook bend, rib and anchor the strip from the bend to the eye. Stroke the hair up and wiggle the wire through the hair so as not to bind too much hair down with the rib. Tie off the wire rib and clip excess.

4. Pull off some hackle fibers for the throat and attach them opposite from the rabbit strip wing. Attach one strip of holographic tinsel down each side of the fly, extending down past the bend about one-half inch. Whip finish.

Remember as you tie this fly that the use of the lead eyes serves two functions: they provide weight, and they flip the fly "upside down" so the point travels above the hook shank. This helps let the fly slide over and around all manner of hook-grabbing obstacles.

This fly is very effectively fished by itself or in conjunction with a nymph trailer. Each fly serves a particular purpose when you are fishing multiple rigs. Jarrett likes to dead drift it through the first half of the drift, then start fishing it more actively once the flies get directly across and start to swing downstream. That way you get the wounded minnow with the nymph in shock, plus the healthy minnow with the emerging caddis. Long before he knew Jarrett, Bill was fishing olive Zonkers in the Wind River range and catching some very large trout. He'd like to try some with the holographic tubing they've got out now.

Pike Streamer
Wes Hibner

Hook: 3X long streamer hook, size 2
Thread: Single-strand white floss
Weight: 0.035" wire
Tail: White bucktail, silver crystal flash, and paired white
    saddle hackles
Body: White yarn or chenille
Rib: White estaz or ice chenille
Wing: Paired white saddle hackles, paired pink hackles,
    paired grizzly hackles, and silver crystal flash
Throat: White bucktail

1. Firmly lock the hook in the vise. Wrap fifteen turns of wire weight directly onto the hook in the center of the hook shank. Anchor with a coating of superglue. Allow to dry.

2. Tie on floss and wrap back to the bend of the hook. Select a small bunch of bucktail about 3–4" long and tie in with the

hair butts flush to the end of the wire wraps. Add four to six strands of silver crystal flash of the same length to each side of the tail. Finish the tail by pairing two white saddle hackles with the tips curving away from each other on each side of the tail. The hackle tips should be even with the length of the bucktail.

3. At the base of the tail, tie in the white yarn and ice chenille. Wrap the yarn forward ¾ shank length to make a plump, even body over the wire weight. Tie off and clip excess. Rib over the yarn with the ice chenille, anchor, and remove excess.

4. When completed, the wing should curve gracefully over the body to midway the length of the tail. Tie a small bunch of silver crystal flash as an underwing along the top of the body to half the length of the tail. Pair the white saddle hackles with the tips curving toward each other. If the stems are doglegged, choose two hackles that will both droop toward the hook shank when paired. Tie in the white hackles over the crystal flash, one angled on each side, with the tips reaching a point above and beyond the hook bend to the tips of the crystal flash. Pair and tie in two pink saddle hackles in the same fashion, but cocked slightly higher to allow a little of the white hackle to show underneath. Finish with the paired grizzly hackles, again cocked to allow a little of the other pairs to show. Anchor the hackle butts very firmly with a few floss wraps and cement the base of the hackles.

5. Take a very small bunch of white bucktail and tie in on the underside of the hook as a throat, the hair just reaching the hook point. Carefully trim the hair butts well away from the hook eye.

6. Finish the fly by making a smooth, tapered head of floss.

No doubt about it, this is a big fly. It should measure 5–8" long when completed because no mere insect will serve as proper pike enticement. Pike are predators and the bigger the prey, the more interesting the response. A change in casting style is also recommended; you want to keep this fly well away from any part of your body when casting. A heavier, faster-line-speed rod will make lifting this fly from the water a safer, easier activity. Big roll casts may be the easiest way of handling the heft.

Getting the hackles to lay in smoothly may take a couple of tries and thankfully, pike are not too fussy about the niceties. But a good wing will move well in the water, and is worth the extra attention. And besides, it looks nicer. Be sure to leave adequate space behind the hook eye to attach the throat and still form a nice floss head.

Variations you might consider include using a lead eye to flip the hook point up (mount the hook in the vise point up to tie the pattern), or adding a monofilament weed guard. Hang-ups are mostly not a problem in the water of the Rio Grande, but if you take it to weedy Springer Lake in April, you may wish to make a few changes.

Wes has been successfully fishing for Rio Grande pike with this pattern (and minor variations) for several years. It likely imitates a rainbow trout, which is a favored pike food.

Bead Damsel

Stan Evans

Hook: 4X long streamer, straight eye, size 14–6
Thread: Olive 6/0
Tail: Olive marabou and pearl crystal flash
Body: Stacked beads, black, blue, and clear, followed by
    all green
Rib: Tag end of thread
Hackle: Grizzly dyed olive.

1. Stack the beads on hook so they appear from eye to bend in this order: black, sapphire blue, clear, then all greens. Leave from ⅛" to ³⁄₁₆" of shank showing to allow for attaching the tail or placing hackle between beads. You may use smaller beads after the first four if you wish the body to have a taper.

2. Attach the thread between the beads and the bend of the hook. Leave a tag end of thread about 10" long to rib the hackle.

3. Pull off a small bundle of marabou fibers from the stem. Keeping it bundled up, trim the butt ends and tie in the bundle so that the marabou fuzz does not get up on the beads. Tie in a few strands of crystal flash the same length as the tail. Whip finish and clip thread.

4. Reattach the thread between the black bead and the eye of the hook. Prepare a hackle by stripping the fluff off the base and tie it in by the butt end, fibers curving toward the tail.

5. Palmer the hackle over the beads back to the waiting tag. Catch the hackle with the rib and palmer the rib forward to the eye. (See the Bug-Eyed Betty description for details on this hackle-reinforcing trick.) Use the tying thread to secure the rib, then clip excess.

6. Whip finish and apply a small amount of superglue to the base of the tail to help keep everything from slipping off.

This fly can be tied two ways. On larger patterns, Bill likes to attach, wrap, and whip finish separate hackles between the beads. This looks really cool, but is somewhat time consuming. On sizes 14–10, Bill likes to leave the long tag end of thread and rib the palmered hackle over the beads.

There are certainly some ways to simplify this fly. For durability and ease of tying, the hackle could just be wrapped at the head or in the thorax region, avoiding the difficulty of palmering the hackle over the beads. Bead pickers that fit over your index finger are useful when threading large numbers of beads such as this fly requires. And be sure to flatten the barb as smooth as possible to avoid fracturing glass beads as you try and get them around the hook.

At one point in time, this fly seemed to be the only one that was working at Stone Lake. Every fly has its moment in the sun, and in this fly's case, it must have been quite the sparkling show! Experiment until you find a technique that works for you—just remember: black, blue, clear, green, green, green . . .

Poppin' Crawdad
Jerral Derryberry and Michael Taylor

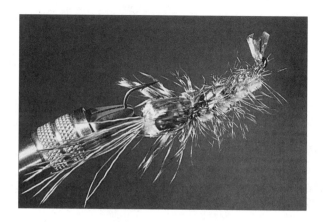

Hook: Dai-Riki 700-B size 2–4, or equivalent 4X long,
   heavy wire streamer hook bent slightly at mid-shank.
Thread: Black 3/0
Weight: Both wire weight and closed-cell foam
Antennae: Natural elk hair
Eyes: Medium monofilament
Shell: Brown swiss straw
Underbody: Grey/cream chenille
Ribbing: Size A monocord
Claws: Long, soft, and webby gray hackle
Swimmerettes: Stiff neck hackle

1. Mount the hook "upside down" in the vise. Tie on the
thread and weight the fly with three shank lengths of wire
weight tied along the shank under the hook as it is mounted in
the vise. Further change the balance of the fly by tying a strip of
closed cell foam on top of the shank.

2. Wrap the thread to the bend of the hook, anchoring the underbody, and tie in ten to fifteen elk hairs for the antenna. These should be as long as the hook shank. Tie in a pair of melted monofilament eyes.

3. Tie in a strip of Swiss straw on top of the fly (which is the usual bottom of the hook) with the excess projecting beyond the hook bend. Tie in a long-fibered, webby, gray hackle by the butt for the claws ¼ shank length from the hook bend. Tie in the grey/cream chenille. Move the tying thread to mid-shank.

4. Wrap the chenille forward to the mid-point of the hook shank and tie off, but do not clip. Wrap five turns of the hackle forward to the mid-point and tie off. Trim the hackle to leave a row of long, soft fibers on either side of the hook.

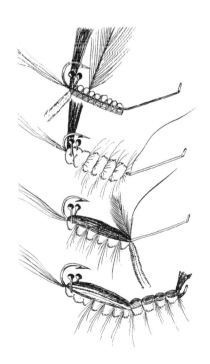

Step 4

5. Tie in the monocord ribbing at the mid-point. Tie in a long-stemmed, short-barbed, stiff-fibered gray hackle. Move the tying thread to the hook eye, then continue wrapping the chenille to the waiting thread, tie off, and clip excess. Palmer wrap five turns of the hackle to the eye and tie off. Trim the hackle below the hook shank to give a flatter appearance.

6. Clip the hackle off the top of the fly. Pull the swiss straw over the top of the fly and anchor at the hook eye. Wrap one turn of monocord over the straw at the mid-point, then rib to the eye of the hook with five turns of monocord. Tie off the monocord and clip both the monocord and swiss straw, leaving enough straw to form a tail. Whip finish and clip thread.

7. Trim the tail into a short, fan-shape. Coat the shell and the whip finish with head cement.

When Karen was a kid growing up in the Midwest, any trip to water—particularly freestone streams—was an opportunity to turn over rocks and poke around the banks to discover the lairs of these strange creatures. And catching them was a challenge. For those who haven't spent any time watching these little space aliens, they employ two speeds: a slow, deliberate forward walk; and a jetting, rearward escape speed that almost defies tracking. By extending and tucking their tail beneath their body in a convulsive maneuver, they "scoot" in rapid but erratic jumps. Unless injured, they are not buoyant, so between scoots they begin to settle toward the bottom. Young or molting crayfish tend to have thinner carapaces and lighter body colors than the older beasts; fish seem to prefer imitations in these lighter colors. This pattern was developed from many discussions of crayfish habits and characteristics by the Rat-faced McDougall Group in Houston, Texas.

This fly is a little complicated to tie, not because of the materials involved but because down is up and the usual head is the tail. If you can keep flipping this thing over in your head to match a visual image of the finished fly, it will help keep you on track.

The down-eye hook with its bent shank and asymmetric weighting is meant to provide a very good imitation of the mud bug's movement. When fished, the fly should be "popped" with a short, quick strip to simulate the flight response. A pause in the retrieve will let the fly flip back over and begin to settle. Another tug will send the fly jumping again, but slightly off to the side.

Although many fly fishers seem to overlook them, crayfish are abundant in many of our area lakes and rivers. Abiquiu Lake, Eagle Nest Lake, and the Rios Chama and Grande are but a few examples where the biggest fish (trout and others) chow down on these crustaceans. Particularly on Eagle Nest, cast the fly into the places where surface debris has been concentrated by the ubiquitous breeze and use a slow retrieve with the occasional pop-and-settle.

Introduction to Wet Flies

Nowadays, true wet flies are the most overlooked type of fly. This is due more to an upsurge in the popularity of nymphing than to a lack of effectiveness on the part of wet flies. Yet on a recent trip to the Bighorn in Montana, a small olive soft-hackle proved to be the most effective pattern; and over a thirty-three year pursuit of trout, the Murderer has caught more thousands of fish for Bill Orr than every other pattern combined.

Whereas the classification of fly patterns into the "dry" category seems easy (hey, it floats!), the distinctions between the subsurface groups are a bit more ambiguous. Most of the old wet flies like those in Ray Bergman's *Trout* are patterns with wings, but included in his categorization are all the salmon flies and many flies with no wings at all that might now be classified as

Murderer

emergers. For our purposes here: If nymph flies imitate the nymphal life cycle stage of aquatic insects, and dry flies imitate the healthy, fully airborne-capable adult, then wet flies might be said to imitate the emergent or crippled adult. Fishing these patterns also follows general rules: wet flies are fished subsurface; dead drift is less important than when fishing nymphs; and the lift of the fly through the water column at the end of the drift becomes even more important than with streamers. Trout will really wallop an emerging caddis or mayfly that they think is escaping.

Unweighted, wet flies are excellent choices for New Mexico's small streams. With moderate weight, they do well as droppers under dry flies. And with lots of weight, they will serve you well on bigger water.

Partridge and Gray Soft Hackle
Bert and Marie Tallant

Hook: 1X long, heavy wire wet fly hook, size 14–16
Thread: Gray 6/0
Body: Dun Haretron and gray fox squirrel mix
Hackle: Gray partridge breast
Head: Thread

1. Tie on the thread and wrap a thread base from the hook eye to the hook bend. Starting at the bend, dub forward with the body material to form a smooth tapered body covering ¾ of shank.

2. Tie in a partridge breast feather by the tip, shiny or convex side facing the hook eye. The feather should be long enough that when the collar is complete, the fibers will reach the hook bend or extend just beyond. From here there are two ways of applying the partridge collar:

A. Wrap a few turns of the soft hackle on edge. Anchor the hackle stem, and clip excess hackle. Use the tying thread to wrap over the hackle fiber butts, forcing them to lie closer to the body. This is the typical way to apply a collar.

B. To achieve a fine collar without the bulk of over-wrapping the fiber butts, carefully groom or fold the feather in half lengthwise, the shiny side of the feather on the outside. Moistening a finger may help. Carefully lay down close wraps of the folded hackle, using both hands to maintain the fold. The fibers should naturally lie close to the fly body. Anchor the hackle stem and clip excess feather. This is the same method used for the marabou Soft Hackle Streamer, and many spey-collared salmon flies.

3. Wrap a small, smooth head and whip finish.

This is one of two impressionistic patterns contributed by Bert and Marie, who've spent some years investigating its effectiveness on many New Mexico waters. Its inspiration obviously came from Sylvester Nemes, the dean of American soft-hackle flies.

It may be fished to imitate a spent adult, a nymphal form, and an emerger—all on the same cast. Its suggestive form lends itself especially well to Liesenring emerger lifts. Bill Orr considers it his fly of choice in sizes 18 and 20 for fishing high lakes.

Bert and Marie have fond memories of catching fish after fish with this fly on a particular summer evening on New Mexico's section of the Rio de los Pinos. The pattern was so enticing to the trout that Bert and Marie continued to fish long after dark, detecting the strikes by feel.

Murderer
Sam Maverakis

Hook: Standard wet fly hook, size 8–14
Thread: Black 6/0
Tail: Grizzly hackle fibers
Body: Black acetate floss
Hackle: Grizzly
Wings: Gray Mallard primary sections

1. Attach thread and wrap back to the hook bend. Tie in a small bundle of grizzly fibers for a tail.

2. Tie in a strand of acetate floss in the middle of the shank and move the thread up about ⅛" behind the eye. Build up a tapered body by wrapping the floss up to the thread, back to the base of the tail, then back to the waiting thread. Tie off the floss.

3. Tie in a fine-stemmed dry fly hackle wet fly fashion (so the hackle fibers project rearward when turned) and take as many turns as you desire. (Sometimes Sam would hackle these flies

fairly heavily and then they could be fished dry with the addition of floatant.) Take just a few turns if you know you're going to be fishing them wet. The hackle should not lay in too close to the body.

4. Mount a pair of mallard quill wings dry fly style (convex against convex), but angle them back wet fly style. Don't wrap back over the rear-most cinch point. That will roll the wings over and away from you. You want the wings to flare nicely from a point directly over the center of the shank.

Step 4

5. Cover up the cut ends of the mallard with the thread and build up a small to moderate size head. Whip finish and clip the thread.

6. Drop a bunch of flies into acetone (nail polish remover) to melt the floss, pick them out with tweezers, and stick them promptly into something to dry. (If your hackle is too soft, it may stick against the body of the fly. An alternative is to treat the bodies, then add hackle and wings. Do a quick whip finish after completing the body, melt the acetate floss, then reattach the thread and finish the flies after the bodies have dried.)

7. Finish by coating the heads with *thick* head lacquer.

Nostalgia can kill you, but when Bill was still in grade school, he caught 168 brook trout in one day on this fly. Sure, none of them were over 13" long, but what the heck. For five or six years, it was the only fly in his box. It proceeded to catch every species of trout in the country, including lake trout. It always seemed to work. There was no need to carry anything else! Then hormones and doubt arrived. Maybe other fly patterns were required? Maybe parents weren't supernatural beings after all? Maybe he should try something else?

A "nymphier" version of this fly uses a dubbed black body without the chemistry of acetate-meets-acetone. However, the glossy, smooth hard body that is achieved makes the fly act differently in water, and certainly makes it stand out in a fly tier's palm. Although acetate floss is getting difficult to find, it may be worth the effort.

Ham and Eggs
Pete Budaghers

Hook: Scud hook, size 12
Thread: Red Kevlar
Body: Red ultra chenille
Egg: Fluorescent orange egg yarn

1. Lash a 1¼" section of ultra chenille to the center of the shank.

2. Lash some egg yarn in at the same point.

3. Whip finish underneath the chenille and yarn.

4. Pull the egg yarn in one direction and cut it with one cut to form the egg.

5. Melt the ends of the chenille with a flame to give it that "natural" look.

So simple it's criminal. We like it as a contrast to the precise, technical patterns some folks think constitutes good tying. This is the Cochiti Lake special. White bass, crappie, carp—none can resist the seduction of the Ham and Eggs. So if you want to catch a lot of fish, ask Pete to show you how it's done. For trout purists, the Ham and Eggs has also caught fish on the Pecos and the San Juan. Go figure . . .

MK Special
Peter Hirsch, Jason Amaro

Hook: 2X long nymph hook, size 6–12
Thread: Tan 6/0 or 8/0
Bead: Gold to suit hook size
Weight: Wire to suit hook and bead size:
#6 hook–3/16" bead–.035" wire
#8 hook–5/32" bead–.025" wire
#10 hook–5/32" bead–.025" wire
#12 hook–⅛" bead–.020" wire
Rib: Gold wire
Hackle: Grizzly
Body: Tan chenille

1. Insert the hook point into the small hole of the bead and insert the hook in the vise.

2. Wrap the entire exposed part of the shank with wire weight, then push the wire up into the large hole of the bead. Superglue the wire to the hook and set aside to dry.

3. Reinsert the hook in the vise and attach the thread between the wire and the bend. Attach the rib in the same small section of shank and put the wire rib in the material holder.

4. Strip off the fuzz from the end of the chenille and attach by the thread core at the bend of the hook. Move the thread up just behind the bead. The diameter of the wire-wrapped shank and the tie-in area should now be about the same.

5. Wrap the chenille evenly up to the waiting thread and tie off. Remove the down at the base of a fine-stemmed saddle hackle. Place the feather on the bench shiny (top side) up, butt pointing toward yourself. Strip the barbules from the right side of the stem. Attach the hackle butt on edge behind the bead so that the top of the feather is toward the bead.

6. Palmer the "half-saddle" back to the waiting wire. Catch the saddle hackle with the wire and palmer the wire back to the waiting thread. Tie off and wiggle the wire to break it at the thread wraps. Whip finish.

Nothing serves to make this fly stand out other than its eerie effectiveness on the The Lodge at Chama lakes and the other fertile lakes of northern New Mexico and southern Colorado. It is merely a tailless, beadhead Woolly Worm in a pale color combination. It is important that the hackle not be too bushy, so palmer it fairly widely over the chenille.

As heavy as this fly is, it is best fished on a floating line to keep it out of the snags. Another option would be to put an unweighted or floating version on a sinking line and crawl it along the bottom.

Pheasant Snail

Paul Zimmerman

Hook: Daiichi 1130, size 10–18
Thread: Brown 6/0
Tail: Pheasant tail fibers and pearl flashabou
Body: Peacock herl and fine brass or copper wire
Shellback: Pheasant tail fibers and five-minute epoxy
Hackle: Brown

1. Tie in thread ¼ shank length from the hook eye, then wrap a thread base back over the shank and nearly halfway around the bend.

2. Tie in two strands of flashabou to form a ½" tail; trim. Move the thread back to the rear of the shank.

3. For the shellback, tie in six to fifteen pheasant tail fibers with the butt ends pointing toward the hook bend. The fibers must be long enough to be lashed down near the hook eye and yet double back to form the shell and a small tail.

4. Wrap forward over the pheasant tail fibers stopping ¼ shank length from the eye, securing them to the top of the shank. Leave sufficient space for the hackle, which will be added later. *Do not trim.* Allow the fibers to project over the hook eye.

5. Tie in a fine wire loop. Tie in six strands of peacock herl so the butts just cover the hook shank. Move the thread back to the rear of the shank, securing the herl butts.

6. Twirl the wire loop and peacock herl to form a snug chenille. Wrap the chenille back to the thread, overlapping when necessary, to create a full, rounded body. Tie off with the waiting thread and trim excess.

7. Fold and pull the pheasant tail fibers over the peacock chenille to form the shellback. "Plump" the fibers and peacock with your thumbs, if necessary, to achieve more roundness. Tie off the fibers, leaving a tail. Whip finish and clip thread. Note you have left space just behind the hook eye for the hackle.

8. Mix a small amount of five-minute epoxy and apply a liberal amount with a toothpick to the pheasant fibers forming the shellback. Allow to dry completely.

9. With a minimum of thread wraps, reattach your thread and tie in the brown hackle immediately in front of the pheasant tail shell. Wrap two to three turns of hackle, then tie off and whip finish.

This is one of those patterns that you must somehow call a wet fly, yet it doesn't easily fit the cripple/emerger-insect definitions. However, fly fishers on Stone Lake and other weedy impoundments would be remiss in overlooking snail imitations.

This straight eye hook (with a very slightly curved shank) should be attached to your leader with a loop. Paul favors a perfection loop for its strength. Dead drifts or *very* slow retrieves will get those fish.

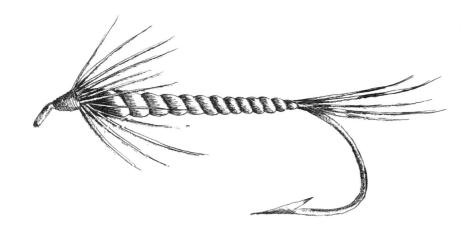

Introduction to San Juan Midges

Welcome to the world of the "midge du jour." The midge patterns on the San Juan are as varied as the tyers who dream them up and anything imaginable can have its moment in the mouth of a San Juan rainbow. For awhile, the hot midge was a couple turns of peacock herl wrapped near the eye of one of those red Daiichi hooks—a perfect bloodworm imitation? Who knows? Described here are patterns that continue to be effective in spite of the ongoing geometric growth of patterns on the river. Basically, tiny patterns in black, brown, gray, red, and yellow will do the trick.

Much more important to success on the San Juan is putting the fly in front of the fish with a dead drift. They are not going to move far to take a one calorie meal, and they may have trouble

Power Baitis

picking your one calorie meal from the ten gazillion meals that are adjacent to yours. Show your fly to as many fish per drift as possible. Good line handling will catch you more fish on the Juan than any magical midge. Invisible flies zipping crosscurrent will just not impress those hard-fished trout.

The rainbows (and especially the browns in the lower river) will chase streamers. They will splash at ant falls and swerve crosscurrent to take an emerging blue-wing olive, but the bread and butter of San Juan fishing is dead-drift midging. Thousands of anglers a year come to this realization. They dream wistfully of the times when other things were happening, but their desire for the big fish will bring them back to their midges.

Princess
Curtis Bailey

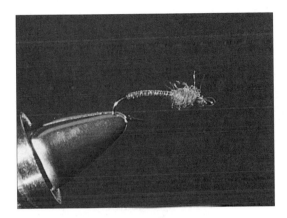

Hook: Daiichi 1273, red, sizes 20–24
Thread: Red 8/0
Abdomen: Pearlescent crystal flash
Thorax: Red superfine dubbing

1. Mount the hook in the vise and tie on thread. Spiral to the bend of the hook.

2. Tie in one strand of crystal flash. Spiral the thread forward to ¼ to ⅓ shank length from the eye. Snugly wrap the crystal flash up to the waiting thread, tie off, and clip excess.

3. Using superfine dubbing, tightly dub a small oval thorax. Whip finish and clip thread.

Like many San Juan flies, this one is "thread-on-a-hook," and easy to tie. The "secret" is the hook: this is a straight-eye, 3X long,

York-bend, red-anodized beauty that shines through the iridescent abdomen and attracts like thread cannot. At this time, Daiichi is the only source so we must all pay their price. When red is the color of choice, this is a good fly to choose.

Use this as the upper fly on a tandem nymph rig.

Secret Weapon
B. J. Lester

Hook: Daiichi 1273, red, sizes 18–20
Bead: (optional) Red midge glass
Thread. Red 12/0
Rib: Extra fine gold wire
Tail: (optional) Tuft of red marabou
Body: Red marabou

1. If you are doing a bead version, insert the bead on the hook, then insert the hook in the vise.

2. Attach the thread, then wrap over the wire rib back to the bend of the hook. Place the wire rib in the material holder.

3. Attach three to four marabou fibers by their tips at the bend, then use the tying thread to bind down the tips up to just behind the bead.

4. Spin the marabou fibers carefully to form a fine red chenille and wrap the body up to the waiting thread.

5. Wrap the gold rib up to the waiting thread and tie off. Wiggle the wire to break it at the thread.

6. Whip finish.

The proponents of the tailed version are also proponents of the bead. They believe that the bead and tail turn this fly into a micro jig that has the proper action in the water.* Non-bead devotees think that the color is the primary seductive element. Regardless, little red things continue to catch lots and lots of trout on the San Juan. Along with the Princess, you should be in good shape.

* If you wish to have a tail, tie in a few fluffy marabou fibers at the hook bend. Pinch them off to be slightly less than one shank length.

Black and Yellow

Garrett VeneKlasen

Hook: Scud hook, size 20
Thread: Bright yellow 6/0
Body: Tying thread
Rib: Black 12/0 thread (on a bobbin)
Wing: Grizzly "pin" feather or grizzly marabou
Head: Oversize black, lacquered

1. Attach the yellow thread near the eye of the hook. Once secure, attach and wrap over the black rib with the yellow thread to the bend of the hook. Leave the rib thread alone while working on the body shape.

2. Build up a bright, finely tapered underbody of yellow. You may want to spin the bobbin at times to help the yellow lay flat. Four passes should be sufficient. Do a two-wrap whip finish near the eye and cut the yellow thread.

3. Rib the black thread evenly up just behind the eye. Do a two wrap whip finish and cut the thread. Do at least a dozen bodies, insert them in a drying board, and lacquer them with clear head cement.

4. Reinsert a dry "body" into the vise and reattach the black 12/0 thread. Attach one of the grizzly pin feathers on top of the shank with the tip extending just shy of the bend. (These feathers are found at the base of the smaller hackles on grizzly necks.)

5. Build up an oversized head, whip finish, and lacquer with thick head cement so that it has a nice gloss.

When Garrett first came out with this fly, he had several versions, including one with a turn of black ostrich at the head in place of the pin feather. Experiment until you find a version you have faith in. The key is the black and yellow body that accurately imitates the larger (female?) midges in the San Juan. Some stomach samples show nothing but these Black and Yellows.

When the fishing turns on, it can be frustrating to tie on new flies, especially if it's cold; hence the need for all that cement work. The black rib will unravel after a few fish if you don't cement it, and you will glue down a percentage of the wings if you try and do it with the wing attached.

Steve, a friend of Bill's, buys this midge by the hundreds, hands them to his clients, and they catch lots of fish. It's been a steady producer on the river for over ten years.

San Juan Adult Midge
William C. Black

Hook: Standard dry fly hook, size 20–24
Thread: Bright olive/yellow 8/0
Body: Thread
Wing: Melted poly yarn
Hackle: Medium blue dun

1. Mount the hook in the vise and attach tying thread. Wrap an even thread base over the entire hook shank. Return the thread to mid-shank.

2. Select a piece of poly yarn half the thickness of the mounted wing. A few fibers are usually enough. Lash the yarn to the hook shank with two tight wraps, then pull both halves upward. Wrap around the base to form a post.

3. Tie in a hackle up to one size "large" for the hook parachute-style with the curve of the fibers down. Wrap two or three turns of hackle, then tie off and clip excess.

4. Whip finish and clip thread.

5. Clip the post to within ⅛ inch of the hackle, leaving only a very short stub.

6. Slip a heatproof perforated plate over the wing stub; the perforation should be just large enough to admit the post.

7. Use a small flame to melt the remaining post into a tiny ball.

Dr. Black is well known in New Mexico and elsewhere as an articulate and avid fly fisher and author. He developed this pattern to imitate those annoyingly attractive adult midges on the San Juan that dominate dry fly fishing in the late Fall. The midges appear to drift flush with the water's surface in large numbers. Tying a parachute with no appreciable wing is possible using the melted poly post as was described by Thomas Olsen in a magazine article, "The Melted Parachute Hackle".

Since the melting part is a bit tedious, tie up a bunch to step 5, then process as a batch. A tin can lid with a small hole punched in it (then reflattened) will suffice for the heat shield.

Chocolate Emerger
Curtis Bailey

Hook: Scud hook, size 20–24
Thread: Dark brown 6/0
Tail: Bronze mallard flank fibers
Abdomen: Thread
Rib: Fine gold wire
Wing: Pearlescent crystal flash
Thorax: Chocolate superfine poly or silk dubbing

1. Mount the hook in the vise and tie on thread ¼ hook shank behind the eye. Tie in five or six strands of crystal flash. Clip the wing to an emerging stub, no more than ¼ inch long.

2. Move the thread to mid-shank. Tie in the fine wire with the excess hanging over the hook bend, then spiral the thread to the bend of the hook.

3. Tie in a sparse tail of four or five mallard fibers. Wrap a smooth thread abdomen to cover the wire and fiber butts.

Spiral the wire forward in four or five turns to rib up to the waiting thread. Tie off the rib and clip excess.

4. Add dubbing to the tying thread and dub behind the wing one or two turns to cover the junction of the abdomen and thorax, and prop the wing at an angle to the hook shank. Dub forward to complete a round, plump thorax.

5. Whip finish and clip thread.

Despite its size, this is technically not a midge but a lovely *Baetis* emerger imitation useful throughout the summer. Keep it fairly slender through the abdomen. Using a 6/0 thread will help make a nicer abdomen, but keep the number of wraps economical elsewhere. The simplicity of the materials allow it to be tied in very small sizes, so it can still be used when the standard Pheasant Tail has become ungainly. It's actually not a bad pairing as the bottom fly of a tandem fly rig with a Pheasant Tail above.

Disco Midge
Curtis Bailey

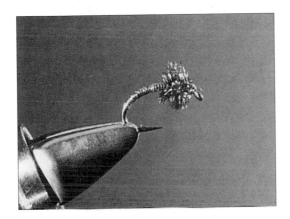

Hook: Scud hook, size 18–24
Thread: Black 8/0
Body: Pearlescent crystal flash
Collar: Peacock herl

1. Mount the hook in the vise and tie on thread. Spiral to the bend of the hook.

2. Tie in a strand of crystal flash. Spiral the thread forward to ¼ shank length from the eye. Snugly wrap the crystal flash up to the waiting thread, tie off, and clip excess.

3. Tie in one strand of peacock herl. Move the thread forward and make four or five turns of peacock as a collar. Whip finish and clip thread.

This skinny, iridescent midge imitation is one of the best for year-round consistency. Variations in the color of the crystal flash range from pink to orange to blue.

Although Curtis does not claim to have invented this pattern, he gets credit for bringing it to our attention quite some time ago. It has become a standard on the San Juan and its fame has spread to other midge-rich tailwaters.

PZ's Fomidge

Paul Zimmerman

Hook: Scud hook, size 18–24
Thread: Black 8/0
Tail: Clear antron
Body: Pearl crystal flash
Rib: 6/0 Black thread
Wingcase: Black closed-cell foam, ¹⁄₁₆" thick
Throat: White ostrich

1. Mount the hook firmly in the vise and wrap a thread base back to the hook bend. Tie in a small piece of antron yarn as a stubby tail, leaving enough length to form an underbody for the abdomen.

2. At the hook bend, tie in a strand of crystal flash and a length 6/0 black thread. Spiral the 8/0 thread forward over the antron yarn to form a smooth underbody. Anchor the antron ¼" behind the hook eye and clip off the excess yarn. Wrap the crystal flash forward in snug, slightly overlapping spirals while

taking care to keep the material flat. Tie off with the waiting thread and clip excess. Add the rib in wider, parallel spirals counter-wrapped over the crystal flash. (This means that if you wrapped the crystal flash over the hook and away from you, then wrap the rib over the hook and toward you. This will help anchor the underlying material.) Meet the waiting thread, anchor the rib, and clip excess.

3. Cut a strip of foam to $\frac{1}{16}$" wide x $\frac{1}{16}$" thick; it will be easiest to handle and least wasteful if you can buy foam the correct thickness and cut strips a few inches long. Tie in the tip of the strip with the excess projecting beyond the tail of the fly.

4. Tie in one ostrich herl, move the thread forward slightly, then make three turns of the herl to form a fluffy throat. Tie off and clip excess herl.

5. Pull the foam forward over the herl and hold tightly while anchoring with the thread. Pull snugly on the tag end of the foam and clip off excess, leaving a $\frac{1}{16}$" stub.

6. Whip finish and clip thread.

This fly is one of a myriad of emerging midge patterns that have found acceptance by San Juan fish. The bluish sheen of the crystal flash, the translucence of the antron, the undulations of the ostrich fibers, and the orientation of the fly in the water given by the foam "head" all seem to give a favorably "buggy" impression to the fish. It is easy to imagine this fly tied in other colors and sizes comprising a significant section of a San Juan fly box.

Power Baitis
Garrett VeneKlasen

Hook: 1 X Long nymph hook, size 24 16
Thread: Black 8/0
Tail: Bobwhite quail feather fibers
Body: Peacock herl stem
Collar: Bobwhite quail body feather

1. Prepare the herl stem by removing the iridescent fibers from the stem. This is easily done by rubbing a soft pencil eraser along the stem. Take care not to fold or crease the stem.

2. Mount the hook in the vise and tie on the thread. Move the thread to the bend of the hook and tie in a small bunch of mottled quail feather fibers for the tail.

3. Tie in the herl stem by the tip, then move the thread forward to the hook eye. Wrap the herl stem forward in even, parallel turns to the waiting thread. Tie off and clip excess.

4. Select a small, soft feather for the collar. Strip the fibers from the base of the feather. Tie in the base of the feather with the curve directed toward the bend of the hook. Take two or three turns of this soft hackle directly behind the hook eye, then tie off and trim excess. Whip finish to form a collar.

With the right materials, this is a simple pattern to tie. And it has an elegant, old-fashioned look that mylar, antron, body lace, and other synthetics simply can't ever match. For additional body colors, use dyed goose or turkey biots substituted for the peacock herl. Quail feathers are chosen because of the size of the soft, mottled tan/dun fibers. The feathers from the leading edge of the quail wing tend to be most suitable for small sizes. Grouse or partridge would be fine substitutes except these larger birds have larger feathers and the collar must be tied with fibers stripped from the stem to get the proper length. Getting a nice, even collar using stripped fibers is much more difficult than turning a hackle. In a pinch, a small dun rooster hackle may be used even though it will not behave the same in the water as a soft hackle.

In the tiniest sizes, this probably imitates a midge, but larger sizes are good *Baetis* or *Callibaetis* imitations. Garrett has taken this pattern all over and found it useful everywhere *Baetis* are present. Have a few in your box next time for the San Juan or Stone Lake.

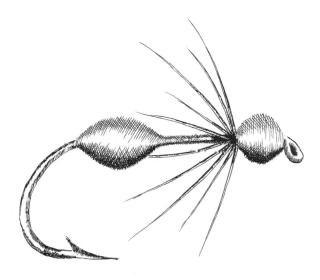

Introduction to Terrestrials

Although these flies might be lumped together with other dry fly patterns, they deserve their own chapter because of the reactions they inspire in fish. Fishing terrestrial patterns can be some of the most dramatic of the season. Trout will often smash a hopper pattern long before and after there are any real grasshoppers along the banks. The trout of the Guadalupe in Texas have such a hankering for fire ants that they actually kill themselves by consuming too many of the toxic critters.

The Rio Costilla has long stretches that run through open meadow and is probably the most popular hopper river in the state. By the time the fishing season opens on July 1, the little cutthroat are focused on anything that falls off the grass and gets pulled against the undercut banks—and that's where a lot of the

Hard Body Ant

fish will be waiting, right up under the banks, ready to dash out for the unsuspecting hopper.

All the small streams are excellent for ants in August and September. The high country lakes are great spots to try both dry and hard body ants. There can be large accumulations of both winged and worker ants on the lee sides of these lakes, and the fish will cruise over there to feed on them. And you will be very happy to find an ant pattern in your box if you are lucky enough to be on the San Juan during one of its legendary ant falls.

Under the right conditions in late June, there can be cicada falls into Navajo and Abiquiu reservoirs, as well as the lower elevation streams in the Jemez Mountains. In the lakes particularly, fish will cruise around looking for these 1" long black meals. Jan's cicada imitation will fool a lot of smallmouth in the lakes and pull some of the larger trout from their lairs.

Fur and Foam Ant
Karen Denison

Hook: Standard dry fly hook, size 12–14
Thread: Black 6/0
Underbody: Black rabbit dubbing
Body: ⅛ inch thick black closed-cell foam
Hackle: Grizzly

1. Tie the thread on behind the hook eye and make a single-layer thread base to the hook bend. Return the thread to a position ⅓ shank length from the bend of the hook.

2. Cut a strip of foam between ⅛- and ¼-inch wide. Tie in the tip of the foam with the excess projecting beyond the bend of the hook. Wrap over the foam tightly enough to secure it to the shank, but avoid cutting the foam. Wrap back to the hook bend.

3. Use the rabbit fur to dub a plump, smooth abdomen forward completely over the foam. It may require two passes with the dubbing to get the right oval shape.

4. Fold the foam forward as for a shellback to the front of the dubbing. Pull tightly for a smooth shape and anchor the foam with two or three overlapping wraps only. Pull tightly on the tag end of the foam and clip off excess as close as you dare to the thread. The butt of the foam will spring back. Wrap over it one or two more times and drop the thread to the hook shank.

5. Tie in a grizzly hackle. Move the thread marginally forward. Take two or three turns of the hackle in one place, then tie off, and clip excess.

6. Repeat the process used to form the abdomen to create a slightly shorter thorax. Make a small thread head and whip finish.

Size 12 and 14 carpenter ant "falls" on the San Juan in June can be a marvelous experience for those lucky enough to be there at the right time. Karen has been fortunate to have had one afternoon on the Rio Grande when there was a brief fall and fish were rising readily to anything that had a defined "waist." More compelling reasons for having at least one ant pattern in your box are the numerous small lakes and beaver ponds in the area. There have been more than a couple of days when the dry flies of choice were either size teeny-tiny parachute midges or an ant of a size you could actually see.

The traditional fur ant has a pleasing shape but takes on water like a sponge after a short time. The foam ants of most books float forever, but look like misfits that should have left the ant gene pool eons before, with square ends jutting out at strange angles. This pattern seems to combine the better attributes of both styles.

It may take a couple of tries to get the proportions right. When tying, Karen often ties a bunch so that the first one that gets flubbed doesn't seem like such a waste. The hard part is preserving a very slender, defined waist. It may help to think of this pattern as two beetles, one slightly larger than the other, completely separated by a hackle. The addition of a small polypropylene wing may make the fly more visible when fishing.

Green Hopper
Ed Koch

Hook: 2X long dry fly hook, size 12–14
Thread: Olive 6/0
Body: Bright olive or chartreuse dubbing
Wing: Dyed olive duck quill segment, treated with
    Flexament
Legs/Collar: Tips of olive deer hair
Head: Olive deer hair clipped

1. Attach thread about ⅓ of a shank length behind the eye and wrap a thread base back to the bend. Dub the rear ⅔ of the shank.

2. Cut out a single segment of treated duck quill and fold it in half lengthwise. Blunt cut one end, and angle-cut the other so that the folded edge is longer. Slip the folded wing over the top of the dubbing with the pointed end projecting just slightly beyond the hook bend and tie in near the front of the body.

Attaching the wing in this manner will help keep the wing from splitting because the dubbing underneath the wing reduces the pinching effect on the wing fiber. Cut off the butt end of the wing and dub sparingly over the thread wraps to tidy things up. Move the thread forward to the bare hook shank.

3. Cut, clean, and stack a bundle of deer hair slightly smaller than a #2 pencil diameter for the head and collar. Position the bundle so that the tips do not extend beyond the bend of the hook. Shorter is probably better. Take three loose wraps over the bundle letting the deer hair roll and flair around the hook.

4. If there is still some bare shank, cut and clean another bundle of hair and cut off the tips. Spin this second little "haybale" of hair between the collar and the eye of the hook. Work the thread through the hair and whip finish just behind the eye. (Depending on how much hair you used the first time, you may not need this second bundle.)

5. Trim the butt ends of the deer hair into a neat cylinder shape, leaving the tips for legs/collar.

This is not an original pattern by any means. It is just a green Letort Hopper. It's included here because it has more than once outfished the Dave's Hopper and Parachute Hopper on the Costilla. This may be because that meadow is full of little green hoppers or because the fisher has more faith in it.

Hard Body Ant
Bill Orr

Hook: Heavy wire wet fly hook, size 8–18
Thread: Black 3/0
Weight: .010" wire (optional on larger sizes)
Body: Lacquered thread
Hackle: Black (dry fly)

1. Attach the thread near the bend of the hook and build up a neatly tapered abdomen of thread. Wrap the body down the bend of the hook slightly.

2. Wrap a single layer of thread up to a point about ³⁄₁₆" behind the eye of the hook.

3. Attach a dry fly hackle wet fly style (fibers curving away from the hook eye) and take a turn and a half of hackle. Tie off and cut hackle.

4. Build up an oversize head that slopes the hackle slightly back over the waist of the ant. Whip finish.

5. Coat the abdomen and head with multiple coats of cement or a single coat of epoxy.

NOTE: For a beautiful, glossy ant, use the melted acetate trick described for the Murderer. Build both the head and abdomen out of acetate floss and whip finish near the rear of the head. Drop a bunch of bodies into the acetone, then put them in a drying board. Reattach a fine thread, attach and wrap hackle. Crisscross the thread through the hackle and whip finish.

Fish in lakes will sprint toward an ant like nothing else. This fly outproduced dry ants and Woolly Buggers at The Lodge at Chama a couple years ago by at least two to one. It is essential for wilderness lake fishing in both Colorado and New Mexico. You want this fly to sink slowly; use an indicator if you must. If you can see the fish coming toward the fly, keep your cool. They will continue to accelerate until the fly is in their mouth, then "airbrake" once they have it. That's the time to tighten up on them. Don't set the hook too hard. There are some big rainbows and cutthroats swimming around the southern Rockies with Hard Body Ants in their lips.

Cicada
Jan Crawford

Hook: Standard wet/nymph hook, size 2 (for sufficient gap)
Threads: Black 3/0, and orange 3/0 or A
Underbody: Black closed cell foam, ⅛" thick
Body: Fire orange ice chenille
Overbody: Black closed cell foam, ⅛" thick
Wings: Pearlescent sheeting

1. Mount the hook normally in the vise and wrap the hook shank with black thread to prevent the body from spinning.

2. Cut two blunted triangles of foam slightly shorter than hook shank and ⅓ as wide as shank length at their widest.

3. Lash the point of one foam wedge to the bottom of the hook shank at the bend, wrapping tightly at the tail end. Secure the tight wraps with a couple of half hitches, and wrap forward with less tension to form a tapered underbody. Whip finish the black thread behind the hook eye and clip.

4. Attach orange thread at back end of body and tie in ice chenille there. Leave the orange thread at the bend of the hook.

5. Spiral wrap ice chenille forward, allowing underbody to show through between wraps. Tie off at head with black thread.

6. With orange thread, tie in the point of the second wedge on top of hook forming a foam "sandwich" and secure at the bend with tight wraps and securing half hitches.

7. Spiral wrap the orange thread forward, using looser wraps to shape a tapered foam overbody. At front, wrap over one side of wedge and around hook shank, then around other side of foam wedge and back to hook shank, leaving outer front corners of wedge exposed. This makes a wide "eyed" head that "pops" when twitched on the water.

8. Half hitch the orange thread at hook eye to secure wraps, then spiral the thread back to tail, adjusting tension to taper the body evenly. Tie off orange thread at tail.

9. Cut a rectangle of pearlescent sheeting ⅓" wide and 2" long. Fold in half to the length of the fly body and cut a long almond shape with a ¼" stem at the fold.

10. Reattach black thread at the hook eye, unfold wing shape, and anchor the wing with two wraps across the fold mark. Refold the wing back over body and wrap two more wraps over the wing "stem" to secure.

11. Half hitch to secure the tight wraps, then make a couple of looser diagonal wraps around hook shank, over wings, and behind exposed foam "eyes" to flatten wings along back of bug. Wrap two more wraps across body and wings at right angles to hook, bring thread forward to hook eye, and whip finish.

12. Cement the wraps at eye and at tail

Jan's Cicada—finished head

Smallmouth bass love this thing. Cast it against the banks at Navajo or Abiquiu and give it a couple of sharp tugs. It should make a satisfying pop on the water that will bring bass charging. Note: The wings buzz when you cast the fly. This helps your fishing partner know when to duck.

Although we've used it exclusively as a lake pattern, take a chance on your favorite late June river and see what happens!

San Juan Worm Life Cycle

T here is one pattern, now a commercially available standard, that has served as the butt of jokes since its introduction many years ago. The San Juan Worm is often the first pattern taught to local fly tying students because of its simplicity and acknowledged usefulness on that tailwater. Mocking the proliferation of highly technical, match-the-precise-hatch descriptions, Bill displayed a concocted San Juan Worm life cycle at our Santa Fe fly fishing shop several years ago, to the delight of many shop visitors. As a lark, we've included a brief revisitation. After all, fly fishing (and tying) is supposed to be for fun.

1. San Juan Worm Mating Pair. This pattern seems to be particularly effective on Friday and Saturday nights. It's especially effective in the stretches near Abe's Lounge and the Sportmen's Inn.

2. San Juan Worm Mating Cluster. Without a doubt, this is the fly of choice everywhere on the river. Note that in the Quality Water you will need to remove two of the hooks and all of the barbs. Tie it directly to the fly line and strip it as fast as you can.

3. Egg-laying San Juan Worm. A Springtime special, it combines the effectiveness of beads with the traditional worm.

4. *Baby San Juan Worm. Like some people's preference for lamb and veal, certain trout develop a taste for the young ones.*

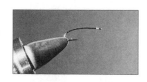

5. *Stillborn Deep Water Emergent Cripple with Trailing Ectoderm San Juan Worm. Sometimes, during those periods of high worm selectivity, you need the ultimate in imitation. The SDWECWTESJW is the fly for you!*

6. *San Juan Worm Terrestrial Mutation. Everyone knows that the San Juan Worm is an aquatic annelid. What many people don't know is that there is a terrestrial mutation present in the river (one of the by-products of that ubiquitous mercury and high levels of dissolved nitrogen). These terrestrial worms like to cling to the willows overhanging the water, much like praying mantids or spiders. From their perches, they snatch unsuspecting insects, other worms, and even small trout. Big browns especially like to dispatch terrestrial worms.*

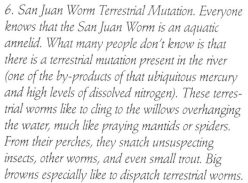

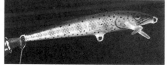

7. *Worm-sucking Rainbow. The fly for double-digit fish on the lower San Juan. Nothing irritates a big fish more than seeing one of its smaller relatives escaping with a snack. Use 0X tippet and practice your oval cast!*

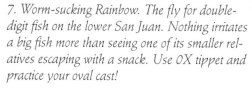

Other Useful Standard Fly Patterns

M**any** widely known standard patterns are quite effective in our area, and we have included here some recipes of the most popular in our favorite colors and variations for local waters.

Dries:

Elk Hair Caddis
Hook: Standard dry fly hook, size 10–20
Thread: Color to match body, 6/0 or smaller
Rib: Fine gold wire or tag end of thread
Body: Dubbing, various colors. Tan, brown, and yellow are most popular for this area.
Hackle: Palmered over the body to match body color
Wing: Natural elk hair
Head: Trimmed wing butt

Royal Wulff
Hook: Standard dry fly hook, size 8–20
Thread: Black 6/0
Tail: Elk or moose
Body: Bands of peacock herl, red floss, peacock herl
Wing: White calf, elk or deer hair
Hackle: Coachman brown

Humpy

    Hook: Standard dry fly hook, size 8–20
    Thread: Tan 6/0
    Tail: Elk or moose
    Back: Elk, deer, or moose
    Body: Red, yellow, or green thread, dubbing or floss
    Wing: White calf
    Hackle: Brown or grizzly

Stimulator

    Hook: 3X long, curved shank, straight eye hook, size 16–8
    Thread: Fluorescent fire orange 6/0
    Tail: Elk hair
    Rib: Fine gold wire
    Rear hackle: Furnace, brown, dun
    Abdomen: Various. Most popular: Yellow, caddis green, or fluorescent fire orange dubbing; "Coachman" peacock herl and red floss
    Wing: Dark or light elk hair
    Thorax: Fluorescent fire orange or amber dubbing
    Front hackle: Furnace or grizzly

House & Lot

    Hook: Standard dry fly hook, size 10–16
    Thread: Black 6/0 or smaller
    Tail: White calf
    Body: Rear half: stripped peacock herl stem
    Body: Front half: peacock herl
    Wings: White calf
    Hackle: Brown or furnace

Parachute Adams

 Hook: Standard dry fly hook, size 8–22
 Thread: Black 6/0 or smaller
 Tail: Mixed brown and grizzly hackle fibers
 Body: Gray dubbing
 Wing post: White calf or poly yarn
 Hackle: Mixed brown and grizzly

Nymphs:

Hare's Ear Nymph

 Hook: 1X to 2X long nymph hook, size 6–22
 Thread: Tan 6/0 or smaller
 Tail: Tuft of hare's ear fur
 Abdomen: Hare's ear dubbing or tan thread
 Rib: Oval gold tinsel or gold wire for small sizes
 Thorax: Hare's ear dubbing
 Wingcase: Turkey tail segment folded over thorax

Flashback Pheasant Tail Nymph

 Hook: 1X to 3X long nymph hook, size 10–22
 Thread: Brown 6/0
 Tail: Ringneck pheasant tail fibers
 Abdomen: Ringneck pheasant tail fibers
 Rib: Fine copper wire
 Thorax: Peacock herl
 Wingcase: Pearl flashabou
 Head: Brown 6/0 thread or copper wire

Prince Nymph
Hook: 1X to 2X long nymph hook, size 8–20
Thread: Black 6/0 or smaller
Tail: Brown goose biots
Body: Peacock herl
Rib: Oval gold tinsel
Wings: White goose biots
Hackle: Brown

Bead Head Biot Stone
Hook: 2X long, straight eye, curved shank nymph hook
    like Tiemco 2312, size 6–10
Head: Gold bead
Thread: Brown 6/0
Tail: Brown goose biots
Body: Peacock herl
Legs: Brown goose biots

Streamers:

Zonker
Hook: 4X to 6X long streamer hook, size 2–8
Thread: Olive or white 3/0
Underbody: Lead tape, or metallic auto tape and lead wire
Body: Mylar piping, silver or pearl
Wing: Rabbit strip, cut "zonker" style, olive or white
Throat: Saddle hackle or tuft of rabbit hairs
Eyes: Optional

San Juan Specials:

San Juan Worm
Hook: Scud hook, size 10–18
Thread: 6/0 to match body color
Body: Ultra chenille or tanned chamois strip, any color
(Most popular: tan, orange, red, pale and bright pink)

Brassie
Hook: Scud or nymph hook, size 16–22
Thread: Black 6/0 or smaller
Abdomen: Copper wire
Head: Peacock herl, muskrat or rabbit dubbing

WD–40
Hook: Scud hook, size 18–24
Thread: 6/0 or smaller, color to suit
Tail: Bronze mallard or mallard flank fibers
Abdomen: Thread
Thorax: Dubbing, various colors: tan, brown, gray, olive, or black
Wingcase: Butts of the mallard fibers used as the tail
Head: Thread

RS2
Hook: Straight eye midge hook, size 18–26
Thread: Gray 6/0 or smaller
Tail: Dun microfibbets or split moose hairs
Abdomen: Thread or sparse gray dubbing
Wing: Tuft of gray marabou
Thorax: Gray dubbing

Index